UNCLE MORT'S NORTH COUNTRY

Peter Tinniswood was born in Liverpool.
He is the author of the bestselling Arrow
titles *Tales From a Long Room* and *More
Tales From a Long Room* as well as several
highly praised novels. He has also written
extensively for television and his credits
include the classic BBC comedy series *I
Didn't Know You Cared*.

UNCLE MORT'S NORTH COUNTRY

Peter Tinniswood

Illustrated by John Ireland

ARROW BOOKS

*For my good friend, Clive Frith,
journalist, and true northerner*

Arrow Books Limited
62-65 Chandos Place, London WC2N 4NW

An imprint of Century Hutchinson Limited

London Melbourne Sydney Auckland
Johannesburg and agencies throughout
the world

First published in Great Britain by Pavilion Books Ltd
in association with Michael Joseph Ltd 1986

Arrow edition 1987

© Peter Tinniswood 1986

Printed and bound in Great Britain by
Anchor Brendon Limited, Tiptree, Essex

ISBN 0 09 954140 8

CONTENTS

CARTER BRANDON was given a week off work.

So he decided he would spend the time taking day trips in his car.

Uncle Mort went with him.

This is what happened.

PAR FOR THE COURSE

IT WAS AN ancient Ford Zodiac with sad headlamps and limp seat belts.

The colour was light blue and cream.

There were bubbles of rust on the bonnet.

'Shall I sit in the front seat?' said Uncle Mort.

'Please yourself,' said Carter Brandon. The sun cowered behind soaring banks of gaunt-cheeked clouds.

A blackbird chackered its alarm.

It was nine o'clock in the morning, and the spring was fitful and timid.

'Where are we going?' said Uncle Mort.

'I don't know,' said Carter Brandon. 'We'll go where the car takes us, shall we?'

With a buck and a bounce and an apologetic twitch the old Ford Zodiac set off, and Uncle Mort allowed himself a gentle scowl and settled into the musty depths of the back seat.

They turned into Derbyshire Road. They swung left at the lights into Halifax Road with its buckle-fronted shops, its snickering second-hand car lots and its Somalis with proud backs.

And down below them the city fidgeted in the fat thighs of the moorland hills.

On they went past the Old Moffat Street tram sheds, bone-rattling across the cobbles of the canal bridge and turning their backs on the old church of The Blessed Martyrs marooned in the cobweb of flyover and underpass.

'Did your mother pack us up for dinner?' said Uncle Mort.

'Yes,' said Carter Brandon. 'Potted meat, bread, cakes and Unsworth's pork pies.'

Uncle Mort nodded.

'Aye,' he said. 'Life can be quite rewarding at times.'

By the time they reached Wilson's Bar he was snoring peacefully, and the wipers were wagging their balding heads at a thin-lipped drizzle.

The dreams of an old man:

Factory girls six abreast on the pavement, cardboard gaiters round their legs, mottled forearms and bold, thirsty eyes. Flat-capped trams with the clatter clatter of wooden seats reversed at the terminus, the flickerless hiss of gaslight, hungry, street corner dogs, tubs of butter, sharp sleek sluck of bacon slicer, barbers with wall eyes and the ragged roses of sooty municipal parks.

More dreams of an old man:

High fells and curlew call, bleat of gritty sheep, go-back, go-back of frightened grouse, fulmars winging the stiff cliffs, flare and trill of startled redshank, drystone walls, mill race and peaty bog.

The car ran out of petrol two miles outside the city boundary.

Carter Brandon shook Uncle Mort to rouse him.

'What's to do?' said Uncle Mort.

'We've run out of petrol,' said Carter Brandon.

'Well, it's par for the course, is that, isn't it?' said Uncle Mort.

There was a plantation of fir and a shallow reservoir with earthen walls.

In the lay-by was a mound of winter grit and a stamped-down beer can.

'I'd best take a walk and see if I can find a garage,' said Carter Brandon.

'I'll come with you,' said Uncle Mort. 'We might find a pub as well.'

Rooks cawed as they set off up the long, slow toil of the hill.

Behind them in the distance the city stretched out its stiff limbs to the first of the morning sun.

The stricken city with its broken-backed factories and the bored chirrup of sparrows, lock gates rotten and askew, blind cinema palaces, terraced houses furrowing the hills, sodden launderettes, takeaway shops with flat-faced Chinese, dull eyes, smokers' coughs, shiftless feet.

They reached the brow of the hill and the road squeezed itself round a barren outcrop of gritstone and there ahead of them was a stone barn, a filling station, a workman's caravan with iron wheels and chimney and a pub.

'This is what I call a good day out,' said Uncle Mort, and they lengthened their stride and wheeled into the pub with a spring to their step.

As soon as they entered the bar a collie dog, which had been slumbering in front of a clinkered fire, jumped up and nipped Carter Brandon on the rim of his right nostril.

Carter Brandon applied his handkerchief to the wound and raised his eyebrows at Uncle Mort.

Uncle Mort smiled.

'Grand dogs, collies, aren't they?' he said.

The landlord pulled them two pints of beer. His neck was scrawned with unshaven stubble and there were aged boil scars, too.

'You're the first today,' said the landlord.

'Oh aye?' said Uncle Mort. 'Well, looking at this ale, we'll most likely be the last as well.'

The bay window of the bar overlooked the stone barn and the filling station. There was a yard with chickens and a Fordson tractor with no seat.

They sat on a bench with their backs to the window and took a tentative sip of their beer.

'It's not bad, if you disregard the taste,' said Uncle Mort. 'Shall we stop on for a couple more?'

'Why?' said Carter Brandon. 'There's plenty of other places. And we've got the whole of the rest of the day stretching out before us.'

'I know,' said Uncle Mort. 'That's what can make life so depressing at times.'

Carter Brandon tapped once more at his nose with his handkerchief.

'Is that nose of yours throbbing?' said Uncle Mort.

'A bit,' said Carter Brandon.

'Well, it would,' said Uncle Mort. 'You want to be more careful where you put it next time.'

The collie dog snapped at a drowsy fly. A stout woman in a dressing-gown and perspiring carpet slippers shuffled out of a door marked 'Private' and whispered fiercely to the landlord.

He turned to Uncle Mort and Carter Brandon and said:

'I'm just nipping upstairs a minute. If you want owt else, you'll have to wait. And don't nick nothing while I'm gone.'

'There's nowt worth nicking,' said Uncle Mort. 'Bugger off and leave us in peace.'

There were clusters of damp, decaying toadstools on the bare floorboards beneath the bay window. Thick layers of dust covered the jar of pickled eggs on the bar. The wind whimpered down the chimney.

Uncle Mort took another sip of his beer, yawned and said:

'I've been to this pub before.'

'Mm,' said Carter Brandon, gently fingering the rim of his nostril.

'Three times as a matter of fact,' said Uncle Mort. 'Years and years ago it were.'

'Mm,' said Carter Brandon, and he yawned too.

Uncle Mort took off his cap, scratched the top of his pate, examined the tip of the finger he had used for the operation and sucked it noisily.

'I've remembered something else, too.'

'Have you?' said Carter Brandon.

'Aye,' said Uncle Mort. 'Every time I were here somebody died.'

'Mm,' said Carter Brandon, and he brushed a fleck of cigarette ash from the knee of his trousers and commenced to tear little pieces from the corners of his beer mat.

'The first time I come in here we was on the way to Blackpool by chara,' said Uncle Mort. 'The roof started to leak so we stopped off here, and Gertie Forshaw's cousin died of a seizure.'

'That must have put a dampener on things,' said Carter Brandon.

'Not really,' said Uncle Mort. 'It was when we got to Blackpool that the rot set in.'

'Why?'

'The sun never stopped shining. Bloody thing.'

Carter Brandon turned and looked out of the bay window. A grey van with buckled wheels brooded forlornly in the forecourt of the filling station. A thin dribble of blue smoke puttered aimlessly from the yard at the back of the barn.

Uncle Mort yawned again.

'The second time I were here the landlord got squashed under a pile of barrels,' he said. 'And the last time Nellie Watmough's husband from the bowls outing got a bone stuck in his throat and choked to death.'

'Mm,' said Carter Brandon. 'These things happen, don't they?'

Uncle Mort nodded gravely.

'That's what the North was like in them days, Carter,' he said. 'People were always dying. It were a fact of life, were death. People snuffed it as regular as clockwork. They didn't complain and moan about it. They just got on with the job. Not like now. They make a real bloody song and dance about it.'

'Mm,' said Carter Brandon.

'It's reached epidemic proportions in the North now – not wanting to die,' said Uncle Mort.

'Mm,' said Carter Brandon.

He looked out of the window once more.

The thin dribble of blue smoke from the yard at the back of the barn had turned into a thick pigtail of acrid black coiling at the sky.

'I think something's alight,' said Carter Brandon. 'Do you

think we should call the Brigade?'

'Bugger that for a tale,' said Uncle Mort. 'It'd take up five minutes of good supping time, would that.'

He picked up a piece of Carter Brandon's beer mat and commenced to suck it thoughtfully.

'The North's gone to the dogs since my days, Carter,' he said. 'You'd got deprivation then. You'd got poverty and misery and despair. You knew where you stood – four square on your bloody knees.'

The door marked 'Private' opened, and the landlord entered the bar. He examined the jar of pickled eggs suspiciously and then he said:

'Excuse me, but is there a doctor in the house?'

Uncle Mort looked at Carter Brandon. Carter Brandon looked at Uncle Mort.

They shrugged their shoulders and Uncle Mort said:

'Sorry, we're all laymen here as far as I know.'

The landlord shook his head wearily.

'What a sod,' he said. 'The wife's mother's just took a turn for the worse. I suppose I'd better ring for the ambulance.'

'Aye,' said Uncle Mort. 'But don't tell them it's serious or they might think you're showing off.'

The landlord retired behind the door marked 'Private', and they took another gulp of their beer.

'The North's gone soft, you see, Carter,' said Uncle Mort.

'Mm,' said Carter Brandon.

'In the good old days of my youth the North stood unique and solid. It hadn't been polluted by the South,' said Uncle Mort. 'They was real people then. People created in the image of what God intended man to be – bronchial, unpleasant company and congenitally rude to strangers.'

Carter Brandon nodded.

He looked out of the window. There was a pumping billow of smoke above the barn.

'I'm sure that barn's on fire,' he said.

'Well, if it is, it's only par for the course,' said Uncle Mort.

He sighed deeply and continued:

'I blame the telly for most of our ills. It's made us all the same. All these bloody weather forecasters. All these women news readers getting divorced right, left and centre. All those incessant Royal Weddings with their big ears and receding chins. It's all designed to make everyone the identical same as everyone else.'

'Mm,' said Carter Brandon.

'Look at me, for example,' said Uncle Mort. 'I served all through the First World War and could you tell the difference between me and Angela bloody Rippon?'

'No,' said Carter Brandon. 'Apart from your muffler.'

'Oh aye,' said Uncle Mort. 'Mufflers excepted, of course.'

They heard a siren. It belonged to the ambulance which pulled up outside the pub, blue light flashing.

Presently the door opened and a man in a blue uniform and a peaked cap jammed on the back of his head entered the bar and said:

'Is this where the emergency is?'

'I don't know,' said Uncle Mort. 'You'd best ask the landlord. He's upstairs attending to his mother-in-law.'

The ambulance man nodded glumly and said:

'What's the ale like here?'

'Rubbish,' said Uncle Mort. 'There's a much better pub two miles up the road yonder.'

'Just my luck,' said the ambulance man, and he opened the door marked 'Private' and stepped inside.

Uncle Mort looked at his empty pint pot and sighed deeply.

'What's wrong these days in the North is that nothing interesting ever happens,' he said. 'In the old days life was full of interest. There was always something to get your teeth into, something to laugh at – mining disasters, epidemics, mob violence on the streets, mass unemployment, Henry Hall on the wireless. It's not like that now, Carter. Life's no interest whatsoever.'

'Mm,' said Carter Brandon.

He finished his pint of beer and looked out of the window. A lick of fire ran across the ridge of the roof of the barn. Smoke tumbled and surged out of the doors and wrapped itself round the breeze.

'That's not a bad fire there,' said Carter Brandon.

'No,' said Uncle Mort. 'It's not a patch on the fires we had in the old days. I remember the day we had a chimney fire at Number 47. It went up like a tinder box. They all copped it bar the lodger. Mind you, he were a tram conductor, so he knew what to do in an emergency.'

'What was that?' said Carter Brandon.

'Save your own skin and run like buggery,' said Uncle Mort.

They heard another siren.

A fire tender swerved to a halt outside the fiercely burning barn. The firemen climbed out, unfurled their hoses and directed the jets of water on the crackling, spitting heart of the blaze. They were wearing yellow oilskins and they were calm and unhurried.

'Bloody load of pansies,' said Uncle Mort.

'How do you mean?' said Carter Brandon.

'In my day fire engines had bells. Real bells,' said Uncle Mort. 'And the firemen used to have to hang on the side and they wore brass helmets and smelled of strong drink. They didn't always put the fires out, but they was a damn sight more interesting to watch than this lot.'

A second ambulance man entered the bar, carrying a stretcher.

'They're upstairs,' said Carter Brandon.

The ambulance man nodded.

'Enjoying the fire, are you?' he said.

'I've seen better,' said Uncle Mort. 'If you bump into the landlord upstairs, tell him we're dying of thirst down here, will you?'

'Right,' said the ambulance man. 'All part of the service.'

He went upstairs and Carter Brandon returned his attentions to the fire. He saw the roof of the barn cave in with a roar and a cascade of sparks. He saw the old Fordson tractor spin into the air as its petrol tank exploded. He saw the fanning flames sidling towards the filling station.

'Bloody hell,' he said. 'If that filling station goes up, it won't be too healthy round here, will it? We could be fried alive.'

'Mm,' said Uncle Mort. 'Do you like Jewell and Warriss?'

'No,' said Carter Brandon. 'I can't stand them.'

'Good,' said Uncle Mort. 'Neither can I.'

The door marked 'Private' opened and the two ambulance

men appeared carrying the stretcher, on which was a body covered by a blanket. They were followed by the stout woman in the dressing-gown and perspiring carpet slippers. She was sniffling into a sheet of kitchen roll.

They crossed the bar slowly and left the pub. The blue light of the ambulance began to flash as it inched its way past the fire tender and set off for the city.

'Bang goes our lift then,' said Uncle Mort.

They were joined by the landlord who said:

'It's mother. She's passed on.'

'Well, that's par for the course, isn't it?' said Uncle Mort. 'Any chance of some service?'

'Certainly,' said the landlord. 'Same again?'

'Naturally,' said Uncle Mort. 'And keep your thumbnails out of the glasses this time, will you?'

The landlord poured their pints, and they were just about to take their first sip, when a fireman thrust his head through the front door and said:

'I'm afraid I'm going to have to ask you to evacuate these premises.'

'Why?' said Uncle Mort.

'Danger of explosion from the filling station.'

'Bloody hell,' said Uncle Mort. 'Can we take our pints with us?'

'No,' said the landlord. 'It's forbidden to take glasses outside the pub except in cases of emergency.'

Uncle Mort scowled at him, downed his pint of beer in a

single gulp and followed Carter Brandon outside.

The firemen were smothering the petrol pumps of the filling station with foam. They had dragged the smouldering carcass of the old Fordson tractor into the centre of the road. It squatted lop-sided with an embarrassed grin on its radiator. Suddenly the wall of the barn buckled outwards. Warnings were shouted and the firemen leapt back as chunks of masonry crashed to the ground and flames seared the fringes of the sky.

'Shall we wait to see if something interesting happens?' said Uncle Mort.

'No,' said Carter Brandon. 'Let's get back to the car.'

They trudged down the hill. Two fire tenders passed them, sirens wailing.

'What a bloody palaver about nothing,' said Uncle Mort.

'Mm,' said Carter Brandon.

When they reached the car, they found a long line of traffic being held up by a policeman on a motor cycle.

He smiled at them.

They told him they had run out of petrol.

He nodded and walked slowly down the queue of cars and lorries talking to the drivers.

Presently he returned with a can of petrol, which he helped Carter Brandon pour into the car.

'Obliging sod, aren't you?' said Uncle Mort.

The policeman smiled.

He returned to his duties of directing the traffic.

After a while it was their turn to swing the car round and head back to the city in convoy.

A lorry had shed its load of Vimto bottles at Wilson's Bar, so they were forced to make a diversion via 'The Tinker's Bucket', 'The Magnet' and 'The Gaping Goose'.

'Bit of a nuisance, that, wasn't it?' said Uncle Mort as they returned home just as the grandmother clock in the hall wheezed waywornly at the eleventh hour of the night.

They sat in the kitchen and drank a bottle of glucose stout.

'Funny day out, wasn't it?' said Carter Brandon.

'Not particularly,' said Uncle Mort. 'It was just about par for the course.'

During the night there was an earthquake in Peru.

FALLEN COMRADES

**HERE SHALL WE GO TODAY?**' said Carter Brandon.

'I'm not mithered,' said Uncle Mort. 'Anywhere'll make a change from your mother's cooking.'

The car snorted at them sullenly as they drew away from the house.

'Do you like cars?' said Uncle Mort.

'No,' said Carter Brandon.

'Neither do I,' said Uncle Mort. 'They've never been the same since they did away with mudguards.'

The gear lever juddered as Carter Brandon waited at the traffic lights outside the Cordwainers' Hall. An ashtray rattled in the rear of the car.

Uncle Mort scowled at it.

'I wonder who first invented the ashtray,' he said.

'I don't know,' said Carter Brandon.

'Most likely the same bloke as invented the soup spoon,' said Uncle Mort.

'Mm,' said Carter Brandon.

He jammed on his brakes hard at Wilson's Bar to avoid a milk float that swung out in front of him without warning. The milkman smiled at him. He smiled back, but then had to wrench the steering wheel fiercely to his right as an old lady with a Yorkshire terrier stepped off the pavement into his path. He shook his fist at her.

'I don't think Northerners should be allowed to drive cars,' said Uncle Mort.

'Why?' said Carter Brandon.

'Because we haven't got the temperament for it,' said Uncle Mort, and he wrenched the rattling ashtray from its moorings and threw it out of the window.

'I see what you mean,' said Carter Brandon.

Uncle Mort grunted.

'Catch a Northerner being daft enough to break the world's land speed record,' he said. 'Sir Malcolm Campbell – I wouldn't give him bloody house room.'

They drove down the valley road.

There were no steam hammers. The factories had gone. The shops were boarded up. There were no houses.

The scummy river heaved itself over sluggish weirs through meadows of rubble and rusting iron. There was a choked canal with crumbling cinder towpath and oil-prowed swans.

'In my days this canal led to Lancashire,' said Uncle Mort.

'Mm,' said Carter Brandon.

'It were teeming with narrow boats in its prime, was this canal. One road out they carried wool and coal. Other road back they brought cotton goods and scrap metal for the furnaces.'

'Mm.'

They passed a pub called 'The Navigation Arms'. Its back yard wall rippled with the reflections of the canal. A carrion crow preened itself on top of a rope-scarred bollard.

'I tell you one thing about narrow boats,' said Uncle Mort. 'They always carried a particularly nasty breed of dog on board. They'd bite the seat of your arse as soon as look at you. Mind you, so would the women. I once saw one at this lock outside the snuff warehouse. She were stood on the back of the barge with her elbow on the tiller and she were wearing a black shawl and a cloth cap, and she were smoking a cherry wood pipe. And she'd got this old wind-up gramophone, and she were playing a Victor Sylvester record.'

'Was she really?' said Carter Brandon, picking up speed as they curved away from the valley floor and hunched their way through scrubby woods and apologetic hills.

'It made a great impression on me, did that,' said Uncle Mort.

'It would have done,' said Carter Brandon.

Uncle Mort yawned.

'I'd half a mind to ask her for a dance,' he said.

'Why didn't you?' said Carter Brandon.

'Because it were a fox trot,' said Uncle Mort.

They came to the slip off road, which led to the motorway.

'We'll not bother with the motorway,' said Carter Brandon. 'We'll stick to the by-roads, eh?'

'Too bloody true,' said Uncle Mort. 'I can't stand motorways, me. They've been the ruination of the North. Before they was invented we was bloody near inaccessible to the rest of the world. Now look at it – we've been over-run by Spanish juggernauts and Southerners with sunglasses and see-through sandals.'

'Mm,' said Carter Brandon.

They came to a preening landscape of racing stables and lonely fields with Friesian cattle. A gaunt old abbey stood on a hummock, and the flattened corpse of a magpie lay on the roadside, its broken wings flapping in the slipstream of the car.

'Bloody cars – I can't stand them,' said Uncle Mort. 'If I had one, I'd do what old Teddy Ward did with his.'

'What's that?'

'Well, he had this car for thirty-six years, and he loathed it. He couldn't do a thing with it. It were always breaking down and running people over, so he got rid of it.'

'How?'

'He buried it at the bottom of his allotment.'

They came to a small country town.

There were mellow churches and a slow straight river with a small Danish coaster moored at the quay.

The main street was broad and in its centre stood an old

butter mart. There were farmers and abandoned super-market trolleys.

'I feel like a slash,' said Uncle Mort.

'So do I,' said Carter Brandon.

He parked the car outside a tin-roofed Methodist chapel. They stepped out. There was a smell of fresh bread and stale sheep.

A bottle green single-decker bus pulled away from the pavement and fumed its way down the main street.

'Have you noticed something pecu'iar about country buses?' said Uncle Mort.

'What?' said Carter Brandon.

'The passengers always sit at the front and leave the back seats empty,' said Uncle Mort. 'If you're sat at the front, sure as hell they'll park their arses next to you even though there's plenty of vacant seats at the back. Too sociable by half, are country folk.'

'Mm,' said Carter Brandon, and he stood on tip-toe and craned his neck to see if he could spot a public convenience.

'No need for that, Carter,' said Uncle Mort. 'We'll go yonder.'

He pointed to a glum-fronted building hunched between a saddler's and gunsmith's and a Thornton's toffee shop.

Above its front door was a sign which read:

'Old Comrades Club.'

'There you are,' said Uncle Mort. 'That's favourite. We'll go there for our slash.'

'Are you a member there?' said Carter Brandon.

'You don't have to be, pillock,' said Uncle Mort. 'If you're a member of one branch, you're a member of every other branch. It's binding, is that, like the Ten Commandments or the rules of cribbage.'

He took Carter Brandon by the arm and led him into the building.

They climbed a flight of loose-boarded wooden stairs with broad, low bannisters. At the top was a man sitting at a desk. He was eating pickled onions from a jar. Uncle Mort showed him his membership card. The man smiled and said:

'That's all in order. Would you like to sign the visitors' book?'

'Does your pen work?' said Uncle Mort.

'Usually,' said the man.

Uncle Mort took the pen, shook it, held it to his ear, then signed the book.

'Here for the day, are you?' said the man. 'Having a nice time?'

'Mind your own business,' said Uncle Mort. 'What's it got to do with you?'

They walked through a pair of swing doors and relieved themselves in the gents' toilet shoulder to shoulder.

'They don't give you much room, do they?' said Uncle Mort. 'It's a poor look out if you've got a small chopper, isn't it?'

'Mm,' said Carter Brandon.

'That's what I say about country people – too bloody sociable by half.'

They found the bar and ordered themselves pints of beer and whisky chasers.

They sat in a corner under the framed photographs of the Queen Mother and Alex Higgins.

Uncle Mort puckered his lips over the frothy head of his pint, sucked long and deep and sighed.

'Memories, eh, Carter?' he said. 'Memories.'

'What memories?' said Carter Brandon.

'Well, look around you,' said Uncle Mort. 'Take a good long shuftie.'

Carter Brandon looked round the room.

There was a machine for dispensing Rennie's digestive pills. On one wall there was a faded white ensign and a faded poster proclaiming the motto: 'Coughs and Sneezes Spread Diseases.'

Behind the bar were plaques of age-battered warships and a lumpily varnished wooden propellor.

On the bar counter was a large vodka bottle a quarter full of penny pieces and a hand bell made from an old shell case.

'Redolent, eh, Carter,' said Uncle Mort. 'Bloody redolent.'

'Redolent of what?' said Carter Brandon.

'Fallen comrades,' said Uncle Mort. 'The lads who never came back.'

'What from?' said Carter Brandon.

IRELAND

'The wars, soap brain,' said Uncle Mort.

'Oh them,' said Carter Brandon.

Uncle Mort scowled at him and lifted back his head and poured the glass of whisky in a single gush down his gullet. He wiped his mouth with the end of his white silk muffler and leaned forward across the table.

'Did I ever tell you about my service in the First World War, Carter?' he said.

'Yes,' said Carter Brandon.

'All them brave lads cut down in their prime. All those sturdy Northerners wiped off the face of the earth, doomed to spend eternity poking their toes at the roots of the poppies in Flanders fields.'

Uncle Mort shook his head slowly and sadly. A sombre sheen came to his eyes and he sniffed hard.

'Do you like Nat Mills and Bobbie?' he said.

'No,' said Carter Brandon.

'Good,' said Uncle Mort. 'Neither do I.'

He went to the bar and fetched back more beer and whisky.

Two elderly men carrying hollow-cheeked plastic shopping bags entered the bar.

'How's the wife?' said the barman to the less toothless of the aged duo.

'She's gone to Bridlington for the week.'

'My condolences,' said the barman. 'And has she shown you how to work the mangle?'

'I think so.'

The two old men took their drinks and settled themselves beneath a fly-stained embroidered tapestry depicting the surrender of the German High Seas Fleet at Scapa Flow.

'I wonder which lot they was in,' said Uncle Mort.

'Royal Marines?' said Carter Brandon.

Uncle Mort shook his head and pointed at one of the old men who was attempting to open a bag of potato crisps with the thickest blade of his clasp knife.

'It's obvious what he were in,' said Uncle Mort.

'What?' said Carter Brandon.

'The Catering Corps.'

Gradually, as midday sidled in, the bar began to fill up. There were old men with watery eyes and blue-veined noses. There were old men with gnarled knuckles and creaking kneecaps. There were old men with scuffed boots and hang-dog waistcoats.

'Bastards,' said Uncle Mort.

'Why?' said Carter Brandon.

'What are they doing back here?' said Uncle Mort. 'Why didn't they pay the ultimate sacrifice like my lot?'

'What are you talking about?' said Carter Brandon. 'You came back, didn't you?'

Uncle Mort scowled again.

'Aye,' he said. 'But after supping this beer I wish I hadn't.'

There was little noise. Voices were low. There was no laughter. Glasses clinked softly. So did teeth, and there was a steady stream of visitors to the toilet.

'Shall we make a move then?' said Carter Brandon.

'Isn't that typical of the younger generation?' said Uncle Mort.

'What do you mean?'

'Here you are surrounded by your nation's living history. Here before you are the creators of your heritage. You are in the presence of rampant patriotism. And what do you want to do? You want to bugger off to a pub with carpets and calendars of nude women.'

'All right then,' said Carter Brandon. 'Let's stop on and have another pint.'

'Now that's what I call patriotism,' said Uncle Mort.

By the time Carter Brandon returned from the bar with the pints of beer Uncle Mort was sobbing softly to himself.

'What's to do with you?' said Carter Brandon.

'I were just thinking of Sam Chedzoy,' said Uncle Mort. 'He copped his lot at the Somme, you know.'

'Did he?' said Carter Brandon.

'Aye,' said Uncle Mort. 'And so did Wallace Crump, Tommy Burrows, Victor Snaith, Wilf Chadwick, Ernie Atkins, Norman and Sid Ritchings and Lionel Slakehouse with his big ears. I wonder what they'd be doing now, if they was still alive.'

'They'd probably be dead,' said Carter Brandon.

'True, lad. Very true,' said Uncle Mort. 'What a waste of life, eh? Just think what they'd have achieved from life if death had not intervened. Take Sam Chedzoy for example. What a talent he'd got.'

'What was it?' said Carter Brandon.

'Farting.'

'Pardon?'

'Sam Chedzoy had got the loudest fart I ever heard in the whole of my life,' said Uncle Mort.

'Had he?' said Carter Brandon.

'It were a work of art, were his farting,' said Uncle Mort. 'He were a damn good gozzer too.'

'Mm.'

Uncle Mort sniffed back a tear.

'He could have gone to the top of the tree in that field, could Sam Chedzoy,' he said. 'And so could Wallace Crump.'

'Oh aye?' said Carter Brandon. 'Was he a trumper too?'

'No. He had this great talent for carving toy soldiers out of cows' shin bones.'

'I see,' said Carter Brandon. 'And could he make anything else?'

'Why the bloody hell should he?' said Uncle Mort. 'If he'd have survived, he'd have made a fortune carving carvings of the Green Howards. He could have become a tycoon with his own chauffeur. He could have had a yacht with masts and gone on continental holidays to Monte Carlo.'

Uncle Mort took a sup from his beer and said:

'And he'd have been unbearable, too.'

'What?'

'He'd have been bloody unbearable, Carter. If you'd gone round to his house and asked him to lend you half a bar, he'd have set his guard dogs on you and damn near decapitated you with his punt gun.

'And mean? Mean wasn't the word for Wallace Crump. When he joined up, he had a full packet of ten Ogden's Golden Tabs in his hip pocket. And I swear to God it were still the same packet he had when he copped his lot at Vimy Ridge. When I smoked the last one left it tasted like a bear's armpit.'

He sighed again and took a slow, reflective pull at his pint of beer.

'Course it were all a great conspiracy, were the First World War,' he said.

'Against who?' said Carter Brandon.

'The North of England,' said Uncle Mort.

'Mm.'

'It were them buggers in the South who thought it all up,' said Uncle Mort. 'All them generals with their boozers' noses and wives with faces like milkmen's horses. All them Tory politicians and Lords and Dukes shooting grouse and wearing women's knickers over their private parts. It were them what thought the war up.'

'Why?' said Carter Brandon.

'Because they thought we was getting too stroppy in the North. As soon as the first Northerner learnt how to open a bottle of cream soda, they thought to themselves, that's it. The buggers are getting too clever by half. We'd best do something about it. And they did. They declared war on the Kaiser.

'And who were the daft buggers what fell into their trap and joined up? The Northerners. Thousands of us. Millions. We took the King's shilling, donned our uniforms and got bunged out to the trenches.

'Millions and millions of Northerners sent out as fodder for the bayonets and the machine guns and the Uhlans with their waxed moustaches and spiked helmets.

'And we died in our hundreds and our thousands and our millions. Draped over the wire of no-man's-land, blown to smithereens in fox holes, spewing out our gore in the cold slucking mud.

'All those lives lost. All them grieving mothers and sweethearts. All that carnage.'

'Mm,' said Carter Brandon. 'And where were the Southerners when all this was taking place?'

'Back home in Blighty sucking Turkish Delight and having their feet massaged,' said Uncle Mort, banging his fist hard on the table. 'You never saw the Southerners when there was trouble. Oh no, the big wigs with their lah-di-dah accents kept them out of it. And why? So that when the war was over and all the Northerners was killed, the Southerners could step in and take over our lands and territory. They'd pillage our cities, defile our womenfolk and make us eat brown sugar and nice food.'

'Keep your voice down,' said Carter Brandon. 'People are looking.'

Uncle Mort rammed the brim of his cloth cap over his brow and scowled deeply.

He was silent for a while and then he said:

'Do you like Abbot and Costello?'

'No,' said Carter Brandon.

'Good,' said Uncle Mort. 'Neither do I.'

The two elderly men with the plastic shopping bags finished their drinks and made for the door.

'Tarra, Brynmor,' said the barman. 'Tarra, Marcus.'

The two elderly men turned and said in unison:

'Tarra Gordon.'

And they left.

'I once had a tortoise called Gordon,' said Uncle Mort.

'Did you?' said Carter Brandon. 'What happened to it?'

'I don't know,' said Uncle Mort. 'It must have got mislaid.'

The thin-hipped, crotchety clock on top of the butter mart struck one, and they commenced to drink their fourth pint of bitter.

'Did I ever tell you about the football match we had with the enemy at Vimy Ridge on Christmas Day?' said Uncle Mort.

'No,' said Carter Brandon.

'It were rum really,' said Uncle Mort. 'We were sat in our trench minding our own business when one of the enemy stuck his head over the parapet and asked us if we fancied having a football match.

'Well, we thought, why not. We'd nothing much better to do apart from tantalise the horses, and it seemed like a good way of getting our own back for what they done to us at Ypres that night.

'So we rolled up our trousers, put on our tin helmets and went out to meet them on no-man's-land. By God, Carter, they was a ferocious sight. They looked inhuman. Like wild animals. And, of course, we couldn't understand a bloody word they said.

'Any road, we kicked off and that's when the bloodbath began. Their right back! He were a right dirty little sod. He'd a shaven head and scars all over the bridge of his nose and every time you put the ball past him he stuck out his leg and bit you on the arse when you fell over.

'And their centre half were no better. He were another dirty bugger. He were like a giant. A man mountain, Carter. He kicked, and he hacked, and he punched and he butted you in the nose.

'Bloody savages they was. When we brought on the lemons at half-time they ate the lot, skin and pips and all.

'Then came the second half. Talk about carnage. The ref awarded us a penalty when their goalie stabbed Sid Seddon with his bayonet. Well, it were a clear case of illegal play. But would they have it? Would they buggery. They just waded in and threw the whole lot at us. Snipers, machine guns, howitzers, trench mortars – the whole bloody works. Not a thought of playing the ball. They had to get the cavalry in to separate us finally.

'What a mess, Carter. Seven dead and sixteen walking wounded.'

'Mm,' said Carter Brandon. 'And who won?'

'Scotland,' said Uncle Mort. 'They beat us five nil.'

DOG DAYS

I T WAS EVENING.

They had been out for the day.

Now they were sitting on upturned beer crates outside the old railway carriage on Uncle Mort's allotment.

Swallows scudded at the sky. House martins flittered their white rumps. Fieldfare and redwing from far away across the roar and grumpy mumble of the North Sea nested in prim suburban parks and the gardens of timbered houses.

The sun shone.

'I can't stand the sun,' said Uncle Mort.

'Why not?' said Carter Brandon.

'Because it's such a bloody show-off,' said Uncle Mort.

'Mm,' said Carter Brandon.

'The bloody thing comes swaggering into the sky like a Liverpool bucko with a shiny arse to his trouser seat and it screams out: "Hey up, look at me. Look at me, lads. Drop everything. Stop what you're doing and come outside and look at me.''

'Bloody thing. Give me a good thin drizzle any day of the week. A drizzle knows its place in life. It just gets on quietly with its job of making everyone thoroughly miserable.'

'Mm,' said Carter Brandon.

Uncle Mort pulled his cap lower over his eyes and scowled at the sun, which glinted on the buckles of his braces and flashed on the metal badges on the lapel of his jacket.

He sighed.

'Do you like the name Thelma?' he said to his nephew.

'No,' said Carter Brandon. 'It's right wet, isn't it?'

'Course it is,' said Uncle Mort. 'Though on that score it's not in same league as Clive, is it?'

Carter Brandon nodded.

A greenfinch pecked with beady-eyed content at a bare patch of ground just beyond the shadows of uncle and nephew.

Suddenly there was a swoosh of wings and a grey and slate-blue shape swooped low over the tangled hedge. It impaled the greenfinch on its talons. It squatted on the ground, spread out its wings and glared at them with cruel, yellow, piercing eyes. The greenfinch fluttered silently. Then the sparrowhawk opened the great cloak of its wings, launched itself into the air and sped away with the greenfinch dangling limply from its claws.

'Bloody show-off,' said Uncle Mort.

'Mm,' said Carter Brandon.

The sun disappeared behind a stand of slumbering horse chestnuts at the far end of the allotments.

A small long-haired black and tan dog with pointed nose, bandy legs and flopping ears squeezed through a gap in the hedge and trotted across the bare ground where the greenfinch had so recently met its fate.

It saw Uncle Mort and Carter Brandon, stopped dead in its tracks, drew back its ears and wagged its tail furiously.

Uncle Mort picked up a cracked jam jar and hurled it at the canine intruder.

The dog yelped, stuck its tail between its legs and scuttled away into the undergrowth.

Uncle Mort sighed again.

'I like dogs,' he said.

'Do you?' said Carter Brandon.

'Oh aye,' said Uncle Mort. 'I were brought up with dogs, me.'

'Were you?' said Carter Brandon.

'Oh aye,' said Uncle Mort. 'Me dad had a succession of dogs, when I were a lad. At any one time we always had at least three dogs in the house.'

'Did you?' said Carter Brandon.

'Oh aye,' said Uncle Mort. 'Well, me dad reckoned they were a bloody sight more efficient than draught excluders and didn't smell so much in summer.'

'Mm,' said Carter Brandon.

Uncle Mort smiled to himself. His eyes clouded over.

'Aye,' he said. 'I remember the dog we had when I were born. It were a Lancashire setter called Bismarck in honour of the famous German statesman of the same name.'

'That's not a bad name for a dog,' said Carter Brandon. 'Better than Wayne or Darren.'

'Too bloody true,' said Uncle Mort. He smiled again, and he continued: 'We had a Bolton otterhound, too. By gum, he were a right bugger, were Neville.'

'Neville?' said Carter Brandon.

'Aye. That's what he were christened – Neville,' said Uncle Mort. 'By the heck, he were a little devil. I were only two month old when he took me out of my cot by the scruff of me neck and tried to bury me on waste ground outside the public wash house.'

'Bloody hell,' said Carter Brandon. 'And did they find you in time?'

'I think so,' said Uncle Mort.

A spiral of gnats coiled and hissed. A lone, lost herring gull circled aimlessly overhead. An ageing dry cleaner's ticket was snuffled through the weeds by the faint breeze of evening.

'Aye,' said Uncle Mort. 'We had a Wakefield spaniel, too. It had a foul temper, did that Wakefield spaniel.'

'Did it?' said Carter Brandon.

'Aye,' said Uncle Mort. 'It took after me father. It looked like him, too, with its bloodshot eyes and its sticky jowls.

There was only one thing he didn't do, which my father always did.'

'And what was that?' said Carter Brandon.

'Chase motor bikes,' said Uncle Mort.

Carter Brandon took the top off a bottle of Guinness with his teeth and handed it to Uncle Mort.

'Me dad once had a miniature Sheffield bloodhound that could open bottles with its teeth,' said Uncle Mort.

'Did he?' said Carter Brandon.

'Oh aye,' said Uncle Mort. 'And he could open the parrot's cage and steal its cuttle-fish bone. And he could open the door of the meat safe and the lid of the gramophone. He were right clever, were our Nansen. We had to have him put down finally.'

'Why?' said Carter Brandon.

'Well, he started bringing friends back to the house when we were out at the pub,' said Uncle Mort.

He took a long, contented swig from the bottle of Guinness. He smacked his lips.

'Aye,' he said. 'All them wonderful, noble dogs we had – Cumberland whippets, long-haired dalmatians, web-footed sheepdogs, Congleton pointers, Morecambe Bay shrimp-hounds. And they was all true thoroughbreds, Carter, with pedigrees as long as your arm.'

'Mm,' said Carter Brandon. 'I've never heard of them breeds before.'

Uncle Mort scowled.

'Long since gone, Carter,' he said. 'The true dogs of the North killed off by colour television and the advent of one man buses.'

The sun came out from behind the horse chestnuts. Its fierce, strident voice hurled back the sullen Northern dusk.

'Bloody thing,' said Uncle Mort. 'It never gives up trying, does it?'

Carter Brandon grunted and sipped at his bottle of Guinness.

'Do you fancy a spin out in the car?' he said.

Uncle Mort shook his head.

'No,' he said. 'Where I fancy going now has long since gone like the dogs of my youth.'

'And where's that?' said Carter Brandon.

'I'm talking about the neighbourhood where I was born, where I was brought up, where I did all me courting and got married to your Auntie Edna in clean socks.'

'Mm,' said Carter Brandon.

'All gone now,' said Uncle Mort. 'All them back to back terraced houses with the women sandstoning the doorsteps and black-leading the tram lines.

'All them street corner grocers' shops with sweating bacon joints and tubs of pickled walnuts and bare floorboards stained with mouse droppings.

'All them pawnshops and black pudding factories and pubs with cast iron spittoons. All swept off the face of the earth. And do you know what they've put in its place?'

'What's that?' said Carter Brandon.

'A bloody sports centre,' said Uncle Mort. 'A sports centre full of silly buggers playing squash in plimsolls and showing the nicks in their arses playing indoor badminton. What's wrong with kicking a tin can about in a cobbled street?'

'Mm,' said Carter Brandon.

'They were the good old days of the North, them were,' said Uncle Mort.

'I bet they were,' said Carter Brandon.

'You didn't have dogs on leads in them days. And they bloody well bit you regardless.'

'Mm.'

'The sun didn't shine neither.'

'No?'

'Did it buggery,' said Uncle Mort. 'It saved itself up for them idle sods in London with their garden parties and their regattas at Henley for boats and their debutantes with flat chests and carrotty pubic hair.'

'Mm,' said Carter Brandon, and he yawned.

'Are you paying attention to what I'm saying?' said Uncle Mort.

'Yes,' said Carter Brandon. 'It's right fascinating. What did you say you were talking about?'

'The sun – bloody thing,' said Uncle Mort, and he screwed up his eyes and glared at the fiery orb sinking itself slowly into the distant horizon.

He took another sip from his bottle and continued:

'It had no time for us here in the North, hadn't the sun. It were too busy ingratiating itself with all them big wigs in the South.'

'Mm,' said Carter Brandon, and he felt the evening warmth dragging at his eyelids and sidling itself into the coziest corners of his brain.

He stifled a yawn hastily and smiled weakly.

Uncle Mort did not notice.

He was in full flood.

And the swallows skimmed lower, and the house martins wheeled and banked in the chase for sun-sodden insects.

'Do you know where I was born, Carter?' he said.

'No.'

'I were born on the back kitchen table.'

'Oh aye?'

'Aye,' said Uncle Mort. 'Well, in them days everything happened on the back kitchen table. You didn't go into hospital for operations then. You couldn't afford it. You had to make do with the table in the back kitchen.'

'Mm,' said Carter Brandon.

'They didn't have time to side the pots away from the table before I was born,' said Uncle Mort.

'No?' said Carter Brandon.

'No,' said Uncle Mort. 'And me dad were bathing the dog, too. Him and the midwife had a rare old tussle before she could find some space for me mother and me.'

Uncle Mort smiled fondly at the recollections of the past.

'When I were born, Carter, they found me right foot was covered in chutney and God knows where the tea strainer got to,' he said.

Carter Brandon felt another yawn welling up. Sleep clawed at the backs of his eyes. His bones ached.

He shook his head rapidly from side to side and smiled.

'Do you like the name Roland?' he said.

'No,' said Uncle Mort. 'It's almost as bad as the name Anita, isn't it?'

'Mm,' said Carter Brandon, and his chin fell forwards on to his chest, and he sat up on his beer crate with a start.

'I wonder where that back kitchen table is now?' said

Uncle Mort. 'It's probably been sold for a small fortune in some poncey-arsed antique shop. It'll be in some swanky house in London all polished and done-up, and they'll be sat round it talking about poetry and eating Italian food in fishermen's smocks and open-toed sandals.'

'Mm,' said Carter Brandon.

The sun still brayed at them. It still smirked at them. It still snarled and yapped at the whisps of cowering clouds.

'That's all us lot in the North are now, Carter – bloody antiques,' said Uncle Mort. 'We're not real no more to them buggers in the South. Good God if they didn't have us to gawp at there'd be no more television on the BBC, would there?'

'Mm,' said Carter Brandon.

'Do you know, if I were to go to the taxidermist's and get myself stuffed, I'd make a fortune being an ornament in some arty farty Hampstead front parlour owned by a lady novellist with knock knees and a face like the back end of a tram.'

'Mm,' said Carter Brandon.

He yawned again and rubbed at his eyes.

Then he said:

'Do you like Beryl Bainbridge?'

'Who the bloody hell's she?' said Uncle Mort.

'I think she's famous,' said Carter Brandon.

'Oh, is that all?' said Uncle Mort.

Perspiration glistened in the stubble on his chin. It ran down his nose and dropped its golden goblets on to his tightly-coiled white silk muffler.

'The good old days,' said Uncle Mort. 'By God, things was so consistent then. That's what was so good about it. You could always rely on bad weather in the summer, Carter.'

'Mm.'

'You could put your shirt on the motor bike and sidecar not working when we went on a day trip to Bridlington.'

'Mm.'

'We always used to take the dog with us on them days out. And you could bank on it being sick just before we got to the outskirts of Malton. I kept telling me dad it were asking for trouble making him ride pillion.'

He smiled.

'The last dog we ever had before I got married to your Auntie Edna was a cross-breed. It was half thoroughbred mongrel and half Runcorn retriever.

'It were so intelligent, too. When it were poorly we never took it to the vet. We just used to give it a note and send it there on its own.

'It hated the summer, too, did Norbert. That's where I must get it from. In the summer regular as clockwork he used to go into hibernation. Every spring he'd slink into the cupboard under the stairs, and we'd not see him again till the start of next football season.

'He sometimes used to come out for the third day of the Headingley Test, but that were only if Herbert Sutcliffe were playing.'

He finished off his bottle of Guinness.

'When I got married, me mother strung white satin ribbons to his collar and trained him to give your Auntie Edna a horse shoe.

'I'll never forget it. It were so moving. We come out of church and stood in the graveyard to have our pictures took.

'And then mother called to Norbert, and he come slinking up to us. He'd been bathed specially so naturally he'd just had a good roll in a dollop of horse shit.

'Any road he come to us with this horse shoe in his mouth. He stopped in front of your Auntie Edna, he wagged his tail and then – oh God, it were moving, Carter – then he stood on his hind legs and bit your Auntie Edna flush on the end of her nose.

'You know, Carter, it brought tears to my eyes, did that.'

'Mm,' said Carter Brandon.

'We took him on honeymoon with us. He never stopped bloody scratching. And every time your Auntie Edna took an inquisitive tug at my pyjama cord he started growling and when she put the lights out and rattled her curlers suggestively, he leapt on the bed and sat on my chest all night.

'By God, I've never had a week of such good sleeping in the whole of my life.'

'Mm,' said Carter Brandon, and his eyelids drooped and

small nerves in his arms and neck twitched and quivered.

'He came to live with us, did Norbert, after we'd got married,' said Uncle Mort. 'It would have been perfect only he couldn't stand your Auntie Edna's cooking. Finally he did what I should have done – he ran away.

'They found him three days later and I had to go to the police station to fetch him. I'll never forget it. He were there in the cage and when he saw me he looked at me with them great pleading eyes, and he started to howl. I hadn't the heart to bring him home.

'He ended up as guard dog to a herbalist. I wouldn't have minded that job meself only I don't think I'd got the teeth for it.'

He sighed again and looked across at his nephew.

Carter Brandon was sound asleep.

His mouth was lolling open and a dribble of faint snores snickered out of his nostrils.

'You young bugger,' shouted Uncle Mort. 'Can't you keep awake while I'm telling you about the days of my prime?'

But then he looked up into the sky and saw the dark clouds of night gathering and slowly nuzzling the sun below the horizon.

The darkness closed in on the allotment and bats swooped at the echoes of the roosting swallows.

Owls hooted.

And then it began to rain.

The rain hissed through the grass.

Uncle Mort stood up slowly.

He looked down on his nephew sleeping peacefully.

The rain was cascading down his cheeks and soaking into his shirt.

'What shall I do?' said Uncle Mort. 'Shall I leave you or shall I wake you?'

He took off his cap and scratched his pate.

And then the small black and tan dog appeared from the undergrowth.

Its coat was bedraggled, and its tail dragged in the mud.

It crawled on its belly towards Uncle Mort.

Uncle Mort smiled.

'Hello, buggerlugs,' he said.

The dog wagged its tail.

And then Uncle Mort let out a cry of pleasure.

'Dear God,' he said. 'I should have known when I first saw you. You're the spitting image of him, if you disregard your bandy legs and your floppy ears and your pointed nose and your colouring. You must be. You must. You're a descendant of our old Wakefield spaniel.'

He bent down and stretched out his hand.

The dog wagged its tail and very slowly and very deliberately bit Uncle Mort's thumb.

Uncle Mort howled with pain.

Carter Brandon woke with a jump of terror.

'What's up?' he shouted. 'What's to do?'

Uncle Mort smiled.

'I have just had an encounter with the past,' he said. 'I have just stepped back briefly into the dog days of my youth.'

He looked down on the dog.

'Come on,' he said. 'You look famished. I'll take you back home and see if Annie'll give you something to eat.'

The dog threw back its head, howled and fled into the darkness.

MY FRIEND, DORNFORD

THE SUN WAS SHINING.

There was a shortage of rad-ishes.

'Did you know Arthur Scargill had got a twin brother?' said Uncle Mort.

'No,' said Carter Brandon.

'Not many people do,' said Uncle Mort. 'He's the black sheep of the family.'

'Where does he live?' said Carter Brandon.

'Lancashire.'

'No wonder he's the black sheep of the family.'

It was mid morning.

There was not a cloud in the sky.

The Queen was just about to distribute the Royal Maundy.

'Shall we go and see him?' said Uncle Mort.

'Why not?' said Carter Brandon. 'What do they call him by the way?'

'Dornford.'

'What?'

'Dornford,' said Uncle Mort.

'Bloody hell,' said Carter Brandon. 'No wonder he lives in Lancashire.'

And so they set off in the blue and cream Ford Zodiac and made for the high moors.

They passed through cobbled mill towns with streams gnashing their rocky beds and dippers bobbing.

Meadow pipits launched themselves from dry-stone walls and sang. Grey wagtails flickered their tails. High above them in the clear blue sky a jet air liner trailed a wake of vapour and flashed its wings at the sun.

Sheep stood sullen and motionless at the side of the unfenced road and peat bogs brooded at the distant horizons.

And then at the crest of the bleak pass they crossed over the county boundary into Lancashire.

Uncle Mort shuddered.

'Have you noticed how the weather always gets more adverse when you cross into Lancashire?' he said

The soft rolling vowels of the wind rocked the car as they curled their way down into the valley bottom. Now they were in the land of cotton mills. But their great windows were eyeless and their gates hung limply and there was no throb of steam engine or whirr of endless belt.

Carter Brandon dropped down a gear as they fell into line behind a stuttering dry cleaner's van with mud-stained flanks.

He turned to Uncle Mort and said:

'How do you know about Scargill's twin brother then?' he said.

Uncle Mort smiled shiftily and tapped the side of his nose with his forefinger.

'There are certain things in life, Carter, which are sacred and personal between a man and his local fish and chip shop proprietor,' he said.

'Ah, I see,' said Carter Brandon. 'That explains it all.'

The dry cleaner's van turned right into a road signposted: 'To The Youth Hostel'.

Uncle Mort stroked his chin thoughtfully.

'I wonder why he's going there?' he said. 'They don't have shiny suits in Youth Hostels, do they?'

'Not to my knowledge,' said Carter Brandon.

'Rum buggers, these Lancastrians,' said Uncle Mort. 'I bet they've still got nap renewing in these parts.'

A red Ribble bus stood outside a black stone inn wrinkled with ivy. The driver and conductor leaned against the radiator smoking cigarettes.

'What a stroke of luck,' said Uncle Mort. 'Shall we go in for a gill or two?'

'No,' said Carter Brandon. 'We're having a day out. Let's give the pubs a rest, shall we?'

Uncle Mort scowled, and he muttered under his breath:

'That's what Lancashire does for you.'

'Give over,' said Carter Brandon. 'I like it round here. This is the county where Winston Place and Brian Statham was born in.'

'Well, they had to be born somewhere, didn't they?' said Uncle Mort. 'We all have to be sooner or later.'

Carter Brandon grunted.

They drove past a quarry.

They drove through a village with a sombre cricket square and a bold double glazing factory.

'How long have you known Scargill's brother then?' said Carter Brandon.

'Yonks,' said Uncle Mort. 'I've known him since he were a nipper in black pumps. He were a grand little lad then.'

'Oh aye?' said Carter Brandon.

'Aye. It was at his infants' school,' said Uncle Mort. 'He were chief convenor of the ink monitors' committee, you see, and they were in dispute with the management over demarcation with the blotting paper prefects, so he called a strike. The kindergarten come out in sympathy and there was picket line violence with the dinner ladies.'

'Mm,' said Carter Brandon.

'Then he went to the grammar and brought the whole school out over the thorny question of underpants.'

'Underpants?' said Carter Brandon.

'Yes,' said Uncle Mort. 'Well, it were the same old story, Carter – they made them take their underpants off before going into the gym. A flagrant breach of human rights, as you well know. It is inherent natural justice, Carter, that a man, whatever his age, creed, race or political persuasion, has an inalienable right to protect his goolies against the exigencies of vaulting horses. So he declared a strike. It were a triumph. It lasted a year and a half and at the end the metalwork teacher was made persona non grata.'

'That's what should happen to all metalwork teachers,' said Carter Brandon.

'Too bloody true,' said Uncle Mort. 'I blame them for all this current obsession with home improvements and building rock gardens.'

He lit another cigarette and sighed.

'Aye, he were a grand lad, were young Dornford Scargill,' he said, 'But then he went away to do his National Service and it all changed.'

'In what way?' said Carter Brandon.

'You'll soon see,' said Uncle Mort. 'Turn left here.'

Carter Brandon turned left down a narrow, twisting lane tangled with honeysuckle and blackthorn. He crossed a shallow pack-horse bridge, skirted a stone-strewn meadow cropped by a shaggy Galloway bull and there in front of him was a low-slung double-fronted cottage. It was made of stone. It had a slate roof and mullioned bay windows and brass carriage lamps on either side of the front door.

'Here we are then,' said Uncle Mort. 'This is where Dornford lives.'

They got out of the car and walked down a finely gravelled path flanked by neat low hedge of lavender. There was a whitewashed wishing-well with bamboo wind pipes tied to the crossbar with fluttering ribbons.

Uncle Mort knocked on the front door.

There was no reply, so instantly he opened the letter box and bellowed:

'Hey up, buggerlugs. It's me. Uncle Mort.'

There was still no response.

A mistle thrush hurled its song from the top of a sycamore. A blue-tit craftily worked the suppling branches of a ceanothus.

'He'll be in his back garden,' said Uncle Mort. 'Come on, let's go and find him.'

He led Carter Brandon through a wicket gate round the

side of the cottage. There was a water butt, a newly varnished church pew and propped against a wall a railway station sign for 'Barnsley Court House'.

They came to the back garden.

There was a stone-flagged patio stretching out languidly from french windows lined with apricot velvet curtains. There were large wooden tubs and terracotta pots filled with pelargonium, euonymus, holly and bay.

There was a sheening lawn bordered by beds of roses, hebe and hibiscus.

'He's a bugger for flowers, isn't he?' said Uncle Mort.

'Yes,' said Carter Brandon.

And then he saw him.

Standing at the bottom of the garden in a grove of bush apples and damsons and stooping over a beehive was a figure dressed in navy blue fisherman's smock and broad-brimmed hat with flowing veil.

'Hey up, Dornford. It's me,' shouted Uncle Mort.

The figure turned, straightened up and took off his hat.

Yes, there it was – the familiar Scargill features as seen with Sue Lawley on TV. The frizzy hair layered horizontally over the skull, the Bourbon nose, the wet lips, the shifty little eyes, the damp teeth, the incipient double chins and the tendency towards premature shaving.

'Doesn't he look a pillock?' said Uncle Mort.

'He does that,' said Carter Brandon.

As soon as he saw Uncle Mort Dornford clasped his right hand to his breast, let out a sharp squeak of delight and hurried towards him, arms extended.

'Uncle Mort,' he said. 'How lovely to see you.'

He kissed Uncle Mort on both cheeks and said:

'And who's your companion?'

Uncle Mort wiped his face vigorously with the end of his muffler and said:

'This is my nephew Carter. And he's happily married with a wife and no sprogs.'

Dornford shook Carter Brandon's hand and said:

'You're very welcome. Do you like Karen Blixen?'

'I don't know,' said Carter Brandon. 'Who does he play for?'

Dornford laughed.

'Isn't he the spitting image of Mick McGahey?' he said.

'No,' said Uncle Mort. 'He doesn't like maroon scarves.'

Dornford clapped his hands with delight and said:

'Shall we have tea? Home-made scones and a pot of Earl Grey.'

'Never mind Earl Grey, Dornford,' said Uncle Mort. 'Have you got a couple of flagons of strong beer put by?'

Dornford laughed again and clasped his breast.

'Ale I have not,' he said. 'But I can produce a bottle of the most acceptable claret. Do sit down and I'll freshen up and raid the cellar. Isn't it naughty this time of day?'

He motioned them towards the garden chairs on the patio and disappeared through the french windows.

Uncle Mort and Carter Brandon sat down.

'Can you see the family resemblance?' said Uncle Mort.

'Yes,' said Carter Brandon. 'It's uncanny, isn't it?'

'Certainly,' said Uncle Mort. 'It just shows what the Boys Brigade and a course of cold baths can do for twins.'

A jay clattered in the distant woodland. A chiff-chaff sang creamily from deep within the apple and damson bushes. A white butterfly fluttered flimsily above the redcurrants and raspberries.

And then Dornford returned from the house with a tray full of drinks. On the tray was printed the legend: 'Oughthwaites Ales Do You Good – By Gum They Do.'

He had changed out of his fisherman's smock. He was wearing daffodil yellow safari suit, pink calf leather shoes with silver buckles and a lime green silk shirt open to the third button down.

'What the bloody hell do you look like, Dornford?' said Uncle Mort. 'Talk about something the dog brought home.'

Dornford smiled and placed the tray on the table before them.

'Now you've the choice of claret or a rather delicate hock. It comes from Germany does this particular hock, as a matter of fact. So does the red Moselle, which is a happy coincidence, isn't it? Now then, the brandy snaps are home-made and I myself personally have cut the crusts off the cucumber sandwiches.'

Uncle Mort grunted and held up the bottle of claret to the light.

'Is it French?' he said.

'Oh yes,' said Dornford. 'It always is, if you're a wine buff like me.'

He poured out three glasses and, as they drank, a large tabby cat with a mauve collar sauntered on to the lawn and commenced to lick its private parts.

'Dear, dear McGregor,' said Dornford. 'And what news of brother Arthur these days?'

'He seems to be all right,' said Uncle Mort. 'He's been on telly a lot these days. He were on "Blankety Blank" recently. Well, it were either him or Beryl Reid.'

Dornford sighed.

'Doesn't he look super on the telly?' he said. 'So forceful. Waving his arms and punching the air with his fists and looking so concerned and so masculine. Just like Clare Francis, don't you think?'

'Oh aye,' said Uncle Mort. 'Only I reckon he's a damn sight better looking.'

Dornford popped a sliver of cucumber sandwich into his mouth and smiled wistfully.

'Dear Arthur,' he said. 'Such a misunderstood man.'

'In what way?' said Carter Brandon.

'In every way,' said Dornford. 'I mean, do you remember that ghastly miners' strike and that frightful baseball cap he wore from breakfast till supper time?'

'Miners' strike,' said Uncle Mort, scratching his chin. 'Wasn't that when they was fighting for more garage space for their automatic Volvos?'

'Not entirely,' said Dornford. 'It was rather more significant than that.'

'Was it?' said Uncle Mort.

'Oh yes,' said Dornford. 'You see, the media in all its perfidy never mentioned what Arthur really wanted for the miners.'

'And what was that?' said Uncle Mort.

'Better working conditions, of course,' said Dornford, pouring out three more glasses of claret and offering round the cucumber sandwiches. 'You see, it all started at the

Hattersley Main Deep. The conditions were quite frightful there. Arthur took one look at them and he insisted that the shaft be immediately lined with Laura Ashley wallpaper and those tunnel things where they dig out the coal should be fitted with Berber carpets. And he said he'd bring the whole country to a standstill if the pit head baths weren't provided with individual shower caps and complimentary sachets of Badidas.'

'I see,' said Uncle Mort. 'And did he demand a free issue of cake forks for their snap?'

'But of course,' said Dornford. 'And he was terribly concerned about the plight of their families, too. Do you know, some of them couldn't even afford to keep up their subscriptions to The Folio Society and the National Trust?'

'Bloody diabolical,' said Uncle Mort. 'No wonder Anthony Wedgwood–Benn thought of becoming a Socialist.'

Dornford flicked a speck of pollen from his daffodil yellow trousers and continued:

'It's the classic case. Two brothers playing the wrong parts. You see, what Arthur really wanted to be was an aesthete.'

'Well, you can earn a lot of money out of being an aesthete these days, Dornford,' said Uncle Mort. 'Sebastian Coe's earned a stack since he became a professional amateur.'

Dornford nodded his head sadly.

'And do you know what I always wanted to be?' he said.

'No,' said Uncle Mort.

'I always wanted to be the working-class equivalent of Clive Jenkins and be a trades union leader. Oh, if only I hadn't met Sergeant Gallimore during my National Service.'

'Sergeant Gallimore?' said Uncle Mort. 'Who was he?'

'He was in the Intelligence Corps,' said Dornford. 'He was the spitting image of Dame Janet Baker and he took me under his wing at Moenchengladbach and we went on nature walks in the Sauerland and engine spotting at Hamm and brass rubbing expeditions to Soest and . . . oh, if only Arthur had met him, what a difference it would have made to his elocution and his dress sense. What a difference it would have made to the miners, too. Arthur wouldn't have failed as he did, poor dear. He'd have closed all the pits, destroyed all the villages and he'd never have been forced to spend a holiday on the Black Sea ever again in the whole of his life.'

A tear came to the corner of his eye.

Uncle Mort coughed.

'And what became of this here Sergeant Gallimore then?' he said.

'It was awful,' said Dornford. 'He was found dead in a hotel room in Clacton dressed up like Herbert von Karajan.'

'Well, it makes a change, Dornford,' said Uncle Mort. 'He could have snuffed it dressed like Mrs Attlee, couldn't he?'

Dornford nodded and sobbed again. He dabbed his eyes with a maroon and white polka-dot handkerchief.

'Poor thing,' he said. 'Why did he have to leave me everything in his will?'

'You what?' said Uncle Mort.

'He left me this cottage and all its contents and a small annual annuity payable each year,' said Dornford. 'I had to take it. It broke my heart. You see, I always wanted to be Arthur Scargill. I always wanted to be my brother. I'd have made a much better job of it. I'm so much better at

mispronouncing my words than him. My grammar's infinitely worse than his. I'm a much better mimic of the Yorkshire accent. I'm terrific when it comes to looking sincere.'

He began to sob.

He sobbed and he sobbed and he sobbed.

Uncle Mort whispered into Carter Brandon's ear:

'Come on, lad. We'd best leave him to it.'

He stuffed his jacket pockets with three bottles of claret and one of hock and led Carter Brandon back to the car.

In heavy silence they drove away from the house as dusk drifted round the flanks of the Galloway bull and soft owls hooted in the evening mist.

They drank a pint of beer in silence in the inn where the Ribble bus had halted earlier in the day and Uncle Mort said:

'Do you know, Carter, when they was lads, I could never tell the difference between them.'

'Mm,' said Carter Brandon. 'I'll tell you something, too.'

'What's that?'

'I can't tell the difference between them now,' said Carter Brandon.

THE MAN WHO WATCHED THE TRAINS GO BY

L ET'S NOT GO OUT TODAY, Carter,' said Uncle Mort.

'Why not?' said Carter Brandon.

'Well, one of the great treats of going out for the day is stopping at home instead, isn't it?'

'Is it?'

'Certainly it is,' said Uncle Mort. 'Just think what the world would be like if everyone stopped at home and never went out. Perfection, Carter. There'd be no wars. There'd be no muggings in the streets. There'd be no vandalism and violence. Peace would reign supreme and no one would ever turn up to hear Mary O'Hara in concert.'

'Right then,' said Carter Brandon. 'We'll stop at home.'

'Good lad,' said Uncle Mort.

He mopped up the remnants of his bacon and egg with a hunk of white bread and continued:

'Do you like Doctor Crock and His Crackpots?'

'No,' said Carter Brandon. 'I can't stand them.'

'Good,' said Uncle Mort. 'Neither can I.'

It was half past eight in the morning. It was raining. The radio crackled.

'Right then,' said Uncle Mort. 'Where shall we go?'

'How do you mean?' said Carter Brandon, taking the last mouthful of his fried spam and tomatoes.

'Well, we've got a choice, haven't we?' said Uncle Mort. 'The world's our oyster. We can sit in the back parlour and mither the cat. We can sit in the front parlour and drop ash on your mother's best carpet. Or we can go to my bedroom and do nowt.'

'We'll go to your bedroom,' said Carter Brandon.

'Good lad,' said Uncle Mort. 'I can see you've got the spirit of adventure in you today.'

So they went upstairs to Uncle Mort's bedroom.

It was rumpled and it smelled of hollow chests.

Nailed to the wall above the bed was a forage cap and a pair of puttees.

There was a well-thumbed packet of Pontefract cakes on the bedside table and a desk diary for 1927.

Pinned to the back of the door was a picture of Randolph Turpin.

'What shall we do?' said Carter Brandon.

'I don't know,' said Uncle Mort. 'As I used to say to the wife, there's nowt interesting to do in a bedroom bar sleeping.'

He took off his cap and scratched his head.

'I don't know. Life's one long misery when it comes to having to enjoy yourself, isn't it?' he said. Then he smiled and said: 'I've got it – let's look out of the window.'

'Good idea,' said Carter Brandon. 'That should keep us out of mischief for a bit.'

They looked out of the window.

The back garden was small.

There was a patch of deeply worried lawn. There was the stump of a lilac and a shed with a rusting bicycle wheel hanging by a nail from the wall.

'I can't stand the countryside, can you?' said Uncle Mort.

'Why not?' said Carter Brandon.

'There's too much grass,' said Uncle Mort.

He sighed.

'This isn't a patch on the view I had from my bedroom window when I were a little lad,' he said.

'No?' said Carter Brandon. 'And what view did you have?'

'The marshalling yards.'

'Mm.'

'By God, it were a sight to cherish, were that view,' said Uncle Mort. 'All them coal waggons with the names of the collieries painted on the side. Them trucks advertising Palethorpe's Sausages. The guard's vans with smoking iron chimneys and balconies at back and front. The little black shunting engines huffing and puffing. The clank of couplings. And at night it were all of a twinkle with the lamps of the shunters.

'They had long poles with a hook on the end, did the shunters, Carter. And I didn't half envy them. I wanted to have a pole like that meself.'

'What for?' said Carter Brandon.

'To bang on next door's front bedroom window when they was having their nookie on Sunday afternoon,' said Uncle Mort, and he smiled with reflective pleasure.

'Marshalling yards!' he said. 'There's a right noble ring to them words, isn't there?'

'Aye,' said Carter Brandon.

'Tram depots – that's another one. And then you've got sewerage farms and liquorice stick factories. All them distinctive institutions of the North of England, Carter, and now no longer with us.'

'Mm,' said Carter Brandon.

'Do you know what they've got now where the marshalling yards used to be?'

'No. What?'

'A Shopping Piazza and a Do It Yourself Discount Warehouse,' said Uncle Mort, and he ground his teeth and clenched his fists. 'Do It Yourself? What's wrong with someone else doing it for you? What's so bloody clever about putting up fitted wardrobes? You can never get the coat-hanger rail to stop in place, can you? You're best getting in proper workmen and letting them bodge it up professional.'

'Mm.'

The black and white cat from next door squeezed its way

through a gap in the fence and began to nibble at the scraps of bacon rind Mrs Brandon had thrown out for the birds.

Uncle Mort banged on the window with the flat of his hand, and the cat put back its ears and fled. It jumped at the fence, missed its footing and fell with a clump and a clatter among a pile of discarded plastic plant pots.

Uncle Mort grinned.

'There's something deeply satisfying about mithering a cat, isn't there?' he said.

'Too bloody true,' said Carter Brandon.

The rain began to fall heavily. It sleeked across the window panes. It drummed on the roof of the shed. It hissed.

'Do you know the best thing about the view from my bedroom window, when I were a lad, Carter?' said Uncle Mort.

'No,' said Carter Brandon. 'What?'

'The main railway line.'

'Well, it would be. Forced to.'

'You used to get all the crack expresses on that line,' said Uncle Mort. 'They used to thunder past. They was so proud. They was so sure of themselves. They were black panthers.'

'Mm,' said Carter Brandon.

'Course, it were best at night,' said Uncle Mort. 'I used to creep out of bed, wipe the frost from the window with the sleeve of my pyjamas and look out and watch the trains go by. The engines was all showered by sparks and there was great billows of steam lit up by flames when the fireman opened up the stokehold. And all the carriages would be lit up, and I'd see the passengers sat there, and I'd wonder where they was going.

'Where were they bound for, Carter? Distant isles in the North of Scotland? Big, fat houses in Mayfair? Were they going to spend the weekend with their mums in Newcastle, or were they going to see Cicely Courtneidge? And what about the boat trains? Where were they going on them, Carter? Moscow? Warsaw? Marseilles and the P&O boats to India? Bloody fascinating, eh?'

'Yes,' said Carter Brandon. 'And I bet you wanted to go with them, did you?'

'Did I buggery,' said Uncle Mort. 'Who wants to go to

foreign climes, when you've got all a man could desire at Wakefield Market?'

'You're right there,' said Carter Brandon.

Uncle Mort sighed and smiled his reflective smile once more.

'The thing was, Carter, I couldn't help wondering about all them people on the trains,' he said. 'What was they doing travelling by night? Who in their right mind would travel by night, when you could travel by day and see out of the windows? And where did they come from? Did they live in houses with big back gardens? Did they own a parrot or a mongrel dog with floppy ears? Had their mums packed up sandwiches for them, and had they remembered to lock the front door behind them?

'And put the cat out,' said Carter Brandon.

'Good thinking, Carter,' said Uncle Mort. 'I can see you're paying attention.'

Uncle Mort rooted in the depths of his waistcoat pocket and took out two cough lozenges. They were covered with fluff.

'Do you fancy a Fisherman's Friend?' he said.

'Aye, go on,' said Carter Brandon. 'I've not had one since last November.'

They sucked at their Fisherman's Friends for a while, and then Uncle Mort said:

'I've never told no one this before, Carter, but when I used to watch the trains go by, I made up stories about the passengers.'

'Did you?' said Carter Brandon, wiping the sweat from his brow and the tears from his eyes provoked by the lozenge which stung his tongue and seared the roof of his mouth.

'Aye,' said Uncle Mort. 'I remember one night this train got stopped at signals right outside our house, and I could see straight into this carriage. And there was just one bloke sat there on his own. He were wearing a black coat with a fur collar, and he'd got a black walking stick with a silver top, and he'd a grey Homburg with a purple ribbon round it. And he were all swarthy and shifty-eyed as though he'd done something wrong like Leon Brittan. And suddenly, Carter, he took an attaché case down from the luggage rack, and he put it on his knees, and he opened it. And he took something out, and I swear to God it were a pistol.'

'Honest?'

'Honest. And he held it up and he put it to the side of his head and then ... and then ...'

'And then what?' said Carter Brandon. 'Go on.'

'The signals changed and the train drew off.'

'Bloody hell,' said Carter Brandon. 'That were quite something, eh?'

'Aye,' said Uncle Mort. 'And that's when I made up this story about him. I visualised everything about him, Carter. I let me imagination run riot. It soared. I couldn't control it. It were uncanny.'

'And what conclusion did you reach?' said Carter Brandon. 'What was the story you made up about him?'

'Blindingly simple, Carter,' said Uncle Mort. 'He'd got chronic gum boils.'

Carter Brandon nodded.

'Well, they can be quite painful, can gum boils,' he said.

'Too bloody true,' said Uncle Mort. 'And I made up another story, too.'

'Oh aye?' said Carter Brandon.

'Aye,' said Uncle Mort. 'I caught a glimpse of this woman on the 11.17 to Marylebone, and I let me imagination run riot again about her and me going off together. She'd have had long blonde hair and slim ankles with thin silver chains around them. And she'd have spoken in a posh accent and smoked cigarettes with cork tips covered in lipstick.

'And she'd have come into my bedroom and swept me away in a navy blue Lanchester. And we'd have sat in the back and she'd have fed me fudge from her mouth and taken her shoes off.

'And then we'd have gone to this cross channel port and taken a boat to France in a howling gale and boarded a train and had our tea in the dining car with waiter service.

'And we ended up in this villa in the hills in the South with pelicans in the sea. She were a cracker, Carter. She hadn't got chilblains on her toes. She hadn't got nicotine stains on her fingers or a loud voice and hairy legs. She hadn't got sharp elbows. She'd got washed hair and those nipple things you read about in the Sunday papers. She kissed you and her lips didn't taste of gravy.

'And we lived there in the sunshine with striped awnings and red wine that wasn't Empire and food that was nice.'

'And what happened?' said Carter Brandon.

'She threw me out because of my bad table manners,' said Uncle Mort.

Carter Brandon swallowed the last of his cough lozenge and hung out his tongue to dry.

Uncle Mort took out the remains of his Fisherman's Friend and replaced it carefully in his waistcoat pocket.

Then he said:

'Why people have to travel I'll never know.'

'They say it broadens the mind,' said Carter Brandon.

'Bollocks,' said Uncle Mort. 'All travel does is breed a nation of malcontents. All this obsession with continental holidays abroad on the continent – it's been the ruination of this country. Why go all the way to Spain to be miserable, when you can be miserable on your own front doorstep at Bridlington?'

'Mm,' said Carter Brandon. 'And Morecambe, too.'

'No,' said Uncle Mort. 'Not Morecambe. Moderation in all things, Carter.'

He bent down in front of his bedside table, opened the door and took out a pint bottle of glucose stout.

'Do you fancy a bevvy?' he said.

'Aye, go on,' said Carter Brandon. 'Shall I go downstairs and pinch a hunk of cheese from the fridge?'

'Why not?' said Uncle Mort. 'It's favourite, is that, if you think travel broadens the mind.'

Carter Brandon went downstairs and looked in the fridge. There was no cheese there, so he took seven slices of cold belly pork instead.

When he returned to the bedroom, Uncle Mort said:

'That's a bit skinny, isn't it? Wasn't there no haslet then?'

'No,' said Carter Brandon.

They drank their stout and munched at their belly pork.

'This is what I call a good Northern meal,' said Uncle Mort.

'So do I,' said Carter Brandon.

'That's why travel's buggered up things so much.'

'How?'

'It's made Northerners discontent with their natural unhealthy diet. All this obsession with Chinese takeaways and hamburgers with plastic forks. It's played havoc with culture.'

'Mm.'

'You get bloody Greeks running fish and chip shops and Wops running Italian restaurants. What do they know about English food and the gristle you're sick on in steak and kidney pie?

'If the Queen hadn't travelled abroad on all these foreign tours, she'd never have married a Greek. She'd have married a Northerner and she'd have opened Parliament wearing curlers and wrinkled stockings like all the rest of us.'

'Mm,' said Carter Brandon.

'It's been the ruination of the North, has travel,' said Uncle Mort. 'In the old days we was a race apart unheard of by Disneyland and Cyprus new potatoes.

'And now look at us – reduced to bathing topless with no clothes in Barcelona and showing off our women's arses in American jeans.'

'Mm,' said Carter Brandon. 'Do you want this last slice of pork?'

'Course I do,' said Uncle Mort. 'Don't be so bloody greedy.'

He bolted back the slice of belly pork and wiped his greasy hands on the hem of the eiderdown.

They spent the rest of the afternoon playing dominoes and three card brag for matches.

'Is it time for tea yet?' said Uncle Mort.

'Yes,' said Carter Brandon.

They packed away the dominoes and the crib board and went downstairs.

'Have you lads had a good day out then?' said Mrs Brandon.

'Not bad,' said Carter Brandon.

'Where did you go?' said Mrs Brandon.

'To the back bedroom,' said Uncle Mort.

'You did right,' said Mrs Brandon. 'Well, travel broadens

the mind, doesn't it?'

They had brown bread and kippers followed by lime jelly and custard.

'I could have sworn I had some belly pork in the fridge,' said Mrs Brandon. 'I wonder where it's gone.'

Uncle Mort winked at Carter Brandon, smiled and said:

'Give me time, and I'll let my imagination run riot about that, too.'

BESIDE THE SEASIDE

T HEY WERE ON THEIR WAY to the seaside.

'Do you like the Swingle Singers?' said Uncle Mort.

'No,' said Carter Brandon. 'I can't stand them.'

'Good,' said Uncle Mort. 'Neither can I.'

They entered the outskirts of the seaside watering place, where they were to spend the rest of the day.

They passed gasometers and glum warehouses. There were rows of back-to-back terraced houses with pot-holed streets and bedraggled corner shops. There were mongrel dogs running loose and barking at the wind. There was a large factory chimney sighing with thick black smoke.

'I like all this,' said Uncle Mort. 'The rot only sets in when you get to the sea and the sand.'

'Mm,' said Carter Brandon.

He parked the car in a large, draughty car park. Scuds of old newspaper and sweet wrappings, caught by the wind, wound round their ankles.

The meter rejected his coin, so he said:

'Sod it. We'll pay later, if they catch us.'

'Good thinking, lad,' said Uncle Mort. 'That's always been my philosophy on life, too.'

They shuffled out of the car park, hands deep in their trouser pockets, and Carter Brandon said:

'Do you fancy a pint of nettle beer?'

'Too bloody true I do,' said Uncle Mort.

They found one of the back-to-back terraced houses which had a hand-stencilled sign in the window announcing the sale of nettle beer.

They knocked on the front door and were ushered into the back yard, where the lady of the house poured out two pints of nettle beer from a large blue and white striped pitcher.

Uncle Mort smacked his lips with pleasure.

'By God, Carter, you can't whack a good pint of nettle beer,' he said. 'If they hadn't invented ambrosia, we'd not have been badly done by making do with this.'

'I know,' said Carter Brandon.

'It's the best remedy known to mankind for hang-overs,' said Uncle Mort. 'And it's not behind the door when it comes to promoting good bowel movements.'

The cranes and derricks of a small dock towered above the wall of the back yard, and there were herring gulls preening themselves on the damp-slated roof of the bonded warehouse.

'I could easily stop here all day,' said Uncle Mort.

'You can, if you buy more beer,' said the lady of the house.

'No, ta, missus,' said Uncle Mort. 'I don't think I could cope with the trumping activities it would entail.'

They finished their beer and left the house with a gruff grunt and a curt nod of the head.

'Where next?' said Uncle Mort.

'Shall we go to the sea front?' said Carter Brandon.

'Aye,' said Uncle Mort. 'I don't suppose we can delay the evil moment no longer.'

The sea blast smacked straight into their faces as they turned on to the prom.

It ruffled the plants in the floral clock and furrowed the surface of the rain water dawdling on the buckled flagstones.

Way out to the west on the distant sea horizon a container ship nodded somnolently at the wind-whipped waves.

'I remember the halycon days when ships had funnels in the middle,' said Uncle Mort.

'Mm,' said Carter Brandon.

'They was proper ships then, Carter. They had sharp fronts and heavy rounded backsides. No wonder they called them "she".'

'Mm,' said Carter Brandon.

'They used to fly their house flags on the mainmast. Thos and Jas Harrison – that were a good one. It were this bulbous shaped cross on a white background.'

'Sounds smashing.'

'It were,' said Uncle Mort. 'And the funnel were a belter too. Black with two white stripes and one red – two of fat and one lean, they called it. Very observant, eh, Carter?'

'Too true,' said Carter Brandon.

They hoisted up their coat collars and set off along the prom.

The tide was in and surly breakers coiled round the groynes and wound their backs round the stanchions of the pier.

'I like piers,' said Carter Brandon. 'Should we take a stroll on it?'

'Why not?' said Uncle Mort. 'There might be a pub on the end of it. That's my philosophy on life, any road.'

The wooden planking of the pier was warped, and there were gaps, through which they could see the waves chunnering and chuntering. There was a boarded-up kiosk with a blotchy sign: 'Gypsy Ernie Petulengro – Fortune Teller to the Stars'. And there were faded, salt-spat photographs of David Whitfield and Eve Boswell.

The theatre at the end of the pier was closed. Its main doors clacked drily to and fro to the tune of the breeze, and there were holes in the roof.

'I once saw Robinson Cleaver here,' said Uncle Mort.

'Did you?' said Carter Brandon.

'Certainly. And Anne Ziegler and Webster Booth. And

Gwen Catley, the Welsh nightingale, and Collinson and Breen – "Somebody's pinched me Puddin".'

'Were they good?' said Carter Brandon.

'Bloody rubbish,' said Uncle Mort. 'Happy days, eh?'

They leaned on the railings of the pier.

The great arc of the shallow bay lay preening itself in the sun, purring to the motions of the tide. The mountains of the high fells sliced the contours of the broad, blue sky. A scurry of oyster-catchers flew low over the rim of the strand.

'We used to come on holiday here year after year after year,' said Uncle Mort.

'Oh aye?' said Carter Brandon. 'And did you enjoy it?'

'Good God no,' said Uncle Mort. 'You don't go on a holiday to the seaside in the North to enjoy yourself. You go there as an annual penance.'

'Mm,' said Carter Brandon.

'This is the place where they first invented the plastic raincoat, you know,' said Uncle Mort.

'Is it?'

'Certainly. I used to buy one every year religious, when we came here, and, bugger me, within two days the buttonholes was all ripped and it stank of stale hake.'

Uncle Mort shook his head and flapped his hand idly at a passing pigeon.

'It were the bloody sea I couldn't stand,' he said. 'You had to go in it and pretend you was having a good time. All them bloody crabs and half-digested turds. And the crutch of your cossie always got waterlogged and sagged down round you knees. And when you got back to the shore, you found some dog had pissed on your boots.'

'Mm,' said Carter Brandon.

Uncle Mort extended his arm and pointed towards the promenade.

'The best time I ever spent here was during the last war,' he said. 'All that prom yonder were covered with coils of barbed wire and you couldn't go on the beach owing to mines and these bloody great wooden poles they put up to stop gliders landing.

'All the pubs were closed for the duration. There was just one British Restaurant selling snoek and Woolton pie and the whole place was full of wounded soldiers from the Hydro in blue suits and red ties.

'By God, it were wonderful, Carter. You could really enjoy your misery in comfort.'

A small coaster huffed its way out of the dock away to their right. It was flying the flag of Belgium.

'I wonder why they come here all the way from Belgium,' said Uncle Mort. 'You'd think they'd have better things to do with their time, wouldn't you?'

Carter Brandon nodded.

The coaster curtsied at the last of the incoming tide, and the herring gulls launched themselves wearily from the warehouse roof and wheeled and yapped about its stern.

'I wonder what the captain looks like,' said Carter Brandon.

'I don't know,' said Uncle Mort. 'It's all part of the great unsolved mystery of life, is that.'

They turned and commenced to walk shorewards.

Now the tide was on the turn and a sliver of wet, puckered sand was exposed to the sun. It glistened. A Manchester terrier with a bandaged front paw barked at the water's edge.

'Do you remember Troise and His Mandoliers?' said Uncle Mort.

'No,' said Carter Brandon. 'Who were they?'

'Well, in a manner of speaking, they was in the same boat as Felix Mendelsson and His Hawaiian Serenaders,' said Uncle Mort.

'I see,' said Carter Brandon.

'I thought you would,' said Uncle Mort.

They left the pier and looked landwards at the buildings on the opposite side of the prom.

There was a shop selling novelty rock and giant humbugs. There was a restaurant called 'The Lobster Pot'. There was a tattooist's parlour and an amusement arcade with glum-eyed one-armed bandits.

'Look at it,' said Uncle Mort. 'The whole panoply of unbridled enjoyment.'

'Mm,' said Carter Brandon. 'I wonder if they have Standerwick buses here.'

'No. Ribble,' said Uncle Mort. 'Life's just one long

disappointment, isn't it?'

Carter Brandon nodded again.

'I like bus companies, me,' he said.

'So do I,' said Uncle Mort. 'Here's a test for you. What was the colour of the Wallasey Corporation buses?'

'Daffodil yellow,' said Carter Brandon.

'Clever sod,' said Uncle Mort, and they set off in the direction of The Winter Gardens.

They were still closed owing to the recent winter, but there was a brand new poster outside advertising the imminent arrival of 'Komic Kapers Karnival'.

'Bloody comedians,' said Uncle Mort. 'Why do they always try so relentlessly to be funny?'

'It's in the breed,' said Carter Brandon.

'In that case they want putting down painlessly,' said Uncle Mort.

They had two pints of beer and a pork pie in the Yate's Wine Lodge, and then Uncle Mort said:

'We used to stop here in digs with Mrs Keenlyside. Her husband suffered something chronic with boils, and there was always pink paper covering the top of her coal scuttles. I wonder if the house is still there.'

'Let's go and have a look,' said Carter Brandon.

'Why not?' said Uncle Mort. 'Anything to avoid having another pork pie.'

They left the pub, and Uncle Mort led his nephew down a side street past a bicycle repair shop and a Plymouth Brethren meeting house.

'Do you remember Stanley Mortensen?' said Uncle Mort.

'Yes,' said Carter Brandon.

'Good,' said Uncle Mort. 'There's life in the younger generation yet.'

They came to a small square. There was a cracked horse trough and an Oxfam shop.

They crossed it and wheeled into a long, draughty street with sullen privets and grumbling pavements.

They walked for half a mile and then Uncle Mort stopped in front of a house with a sign above its front door marked 'Villa Rawmarsh' and said:

'Bloody hell, it's still here, and it hasn't changed a bit.

That same old unwelcoming exterior. That same threat of impending mince and carrots. That same old chill rasping out through the letter box. I wonder if Mrs Keenlyside's still there?'

'Let's knock on the door and see,' said Carter Brandon. 'It'll bring back memories.'

'That's what I'm afraid of,' said Uncle Mort.

Nonetheless he walked up the front path and rang the bell on the door.

After a while it was opened by a small white-haired lady with nicotine stains on her top lip and unzipped fur boots hanging round her ankles.

'Mrs Keenlyside!' said Uncle Mort. 'After all this time. Do you remember me?'

'No,' said the old lady.

'I'm the one who was sick in the bath the Whitsuntide of '49.'

The old lady nodded.

'And are you the one what set fire to the coal shed in the back end of '36?'

'No,' said Uncle Mort. 'Culpability doesn't extend that far, I'm afraid.'

From over Mrs Keenlyside's shoulders wafted the smell of grey mince and sodden carrots.

'Do you think we could come in for a bit?' said Uncle Mort.

'No,' said Mrs Keenlyside. 'Guests are not allowed on the premises between the hours of ten-thirty and five.'

'Aye, but we're not guests, missus,' said Uncle Mort. 'We've got more respect for our stomachs.'

'Then what do you want?'

'I had the perfectly normal desire, missus, to show my nephew here the place where I spent some of the most miserable days in the whole of my life.'

Mrs Keenlyside looked them up and down slowly.

Then she said:

'Are you any good at fixing up outside lavatories?'

'Carter is,' said Uncle Mort, and he gave his nephew a sharp dig in the ribs with his elbow.

'Aye, I'm a dab hand at it,' said Carter Brandon. 'I've

got certificates for it from adult education.'

'Right, you can come in,' said Mrs Keenlyside. 'But eating your own food in the bedrooms is strictly forbidden.'

They followed her into the house. The gloom snuffled at their ankles. The damp cowered. She directed Carter Brandon to the outside lavatory. She led Uncle Mort into the kitchen.

'Do you want a cup of tea?' she said.

'Are the cups clean?' said Uncle Mort.

'Not usually.'

'Right then. I'll have a cup of cocoa instead.'

A large black cat with a stunted tail and tattered ears was lying asleep among a jumble of congealed jam jars and overflowing ashtrays on the kitchen table next to a budgie, which was scraping in the bottom of its cage, knee deep in husks and tacky droppings.

'How's your husband?' said Uncle Mort.

'Dead,' said Mrs Keenlyside.

'Boils?'

'No. He caught something off the budgie.'

'I see,' said Uncle Mort. 'And did you go to his funeral?'

'I think so,' said Mrs Keenlyside.

A large, grease-encrusted pan on the cooker began to spit and froth. From its depths there emerged a pulsating umbrella of fatty scum. It quivered for a moment, gulped and then overflowed on to the jet of gas, which sizzled and then extinguished itself with a sickly plop.

'And what culinary delight is that, missus?' said Uncle Mort.

'What day is it?' said Mrs Keenlyside.

'Wednesday,' said Uncle Mort.

'In that case it must be mince,' said Mrs Keenlyside.

She went to the small, narrow window fighting with the dimness in the farthest corner of the room and looked outside into the back yard.

'He's taking his time out there, is that lad,' she said. 'Do you fancy making yourself useful while you're waiting and cleaning out the budgie?'

'No ta,' said Uncle Mort. 'I've not got me kidney donor's card on me, you see.'

She sniffed, and then she put her hands on her hips and narrowed her eyes.

'I remember you now,' she said. 'It always rained when you stopped here, didn't it?'

'That's right,' said Uncle Mort. 'We had hail stones, too.'

For the first time she smiled.

'They don't breed them like you these days, do they?' she said.

'No,' said Uncle Mort. 'It's the younger generation you see. They don't breed old people now.'

She smiled again. And then she began to move slowly towards him.

'Do you fancy a plate of mince then?' she said softly.

A bead of perspiration stood out on the middle of Uncle Mort's forehead.

'Pardon?' he said.

'Have a plate of mince and carrots,' she said. 'It does wonders to a man, does a plate of mince and carrots. Ask Foden.'

'Who's Foden?' said Uncle Mort, backing away from her.

'My husband.'

'But he's dead, missus.'

'I know,' said Mrs Keenlyside. 'That's why I've been condemned by the council this past fifteen years.'

'Pardon?' said Uncle Mort, and he felt a twinge from the incipient rash round his navel.

'They condemned me owing to the circumstances of his death. I've not had no visitors here since the day they took him out feet first in his best chalk stripe trousers.'

She moved even closer to him.

'I've been so lonely,' she said. 'No one to hector. No one to badger. No one to complain about at the dog biscuit shop. No one to watch on the petty early doors. Have a plate of mince. You can stop on illegal, if you like. My terms are very reasonable if you disregard inflation.

Uncle Mort began to move backwards to the hall door, and a flush came to his neck.

'Oh hell,' he said. 'Oh bloody hell.'

And at that moment Carter Brandon entered the kitchen and said:

'Right then. I've fixed it up for you. It was the robins nesting in your cistern what caused the trouble.'

'Good lad,' said Uncle Mort. 'You always was red hot as regards ornithology, wasn't you?'

He took hold of his nephew, steered him though the hall door, pushed him down the corridor and opened the front door.

He turned to Mrs Keenlyside and said:

'If there's anything else of a personal nature you want fixing, missus, don't hesitate to get in touch.'

And he slammed the front door behind them and headed

at pace down the street and led Carter Brandon to the Yates's Wine Lodge, where he downed two large whiskies and a pint of stout.

When he had finished, he looked up and smiled weakly.

'You were in a hurry,' said Carter Brandon.

'I know,' said Uncle Mort. 'I just escaped in time.'

'From what?'

'From her,' said Uncle Mort. 'I reckon she were proposing something of a rather intimate activity between man and woman with your socks off in the best bedroom.'

Carter Brandon smiled.

And then he laughed. He laughed for a long time, and Uncle Mort scowled.

At length when his laughter had subsided he said:

'Why didn't you take up the offer then?'

'Simple,' said Uncle Mort. 'Because it would have involved stopping the night.'

'What's wrong with that?'

'Everything,' said Uncle Mort. 'Tomorrow is Thursday.'

'So?'

Uncle Mort shook his head slowly and said:

'You don't know nothing, lad, do you? Thursday is boiled rissoles and cabbage.'

It was dark, when they returned home.

YOUNG CHOC-OLATE

D O YOU FANCY GOING to a funeral today?' said Uncle Mort.

'Yes,' said Carter Brandon. 'Any particular one?'

'No,' said Uncle Mort. 'I'm not right mithered really.'

They were drinking mugs of tea in the shed on Uncle Mort's allotment. It was a brake waggon from the Lancashire and Yorkshire Railway. They were sitting on its verandah overlooking the allotment with its bounteous selection of weeds in full, riotous bloom and its impenetrable tangles of undergrowth chirring with wrens and whitethroats.

There was not a single flower or vegetable to be seen.

'That's what I call the true face of Mother Nature,' said Uncle Mort. 'I wouldn't mind being buried here, when I snuff it.'

'I'll see what I can do,' said Carter Brandon.

'Ta very much,' said Uncle Mort. 'But remember to keep me out of the sun, won't you?'

He poured himself another mug of tea and slopped into it a dollop of condensed milk from a battered and rusting tin.

'I like a good funeral, me,' he said.

'So do I,' said Carter Brandon. 'Particularly if it's family.'

'It doesn't bother me either road so long as the catering's up to scratch,' said Uncle Mort. 'A duff pork pie is a duff pork pie whatever the status of the corpse you're burying.'

'True,' said Carter Brandon.

The leaden sky was drifting with dumpling clouds. The moon was coy. There had been a frost.

'I like a good wedding on the quiet, too,' said Uncle Mort.

'Do you?'

'Certainly,' said Uncle Mort. 'You can get things off your chest at a wedding.'

'In what way?' said Carter Brandon.

'Well, you can tell your nearest and dearest and your closest of relatives what you really think of them with their swanky lino and their brass stair rods and his habit of picking his teeth with bits of cigarette packets and her bloody awful dress sense as regards clothes and that snotty-nosed sprog they used to have with his transparent ears and his droopy underpants.'

'Who are you talking about?' said Carter Brandon.

'Your mum and dad,' said Uncle Mort.

Carter Brandon nodded.

'Oh them,' he said.

Uncle Mort slurped at his tea and smacked his lips juicily.

'I'm not keen on engagement parties, though,' he said.

'Why not?' said Carter Brandon.

Uncle Mort scratched the back of his head with the sharp end of an aged trowel and said:

'What were the name of that son of mine what got knocked off his bike and killed?'

'Cyril,' said Carter Brandon.

'Cyril! That's him,' said Uncle Mort. 'I'll never forget his engagement party for as long as I live.'

'Why?'

'It were a total disaster,' said Uncle Mort. 'Everyone enjoyed themselves.'

'I didn't,' said Carter Brandon.

'I know,' said Uncle Mort. 'You were crafty and went to the Cup Final at Wembley with me instead.'

'That's right,' said Carter Brandon. 'Who won?'

'I can't remember,' said Uncle Mort. 'Does it really matter?'

Two cabbage white butterflies dabbled above a patch of damp nettles. A kestrel hovered on wing tip threads. A trio of mute swans wheezed their way low across the distant line of houses.

'So which funeral are we going to then?' said Carter Brandon, yawning and stretching his legs.

'I've got the local rag here,' said Uncle Mort. 'Let's see what they've got to offer.'

He opened the paper. He read silently for a few minutes. Then he said:

'I see there's another bull run amok in the ointment warehouse.'

'Mm,' said Carter Brandon.

Uncle Mort rustled the paper and read on, muttering softly under his breath.

Suddenly he looked up and said:

'Here we are, Carter. There's a cracker of a funeral here. Young Chocolate. He's being buried at half past twelve. Talk about falling right into our laps, eh?'

'Aye,' said Carter Brandon. 'Who is Young Chocolate by the way?'

'Let's go to the car and I'll tell you on the way to his funeral,' said Uncle Mort.

They closed up the shed, relieved their bladders among the dock leaves at the side of the verandah and made their way to the car.

'Do you like Revnell and West?' said Uncle Mort.

'No,' said Carter Brandon.

'Good,' said Uncle Mort. 'Neither do I.'

The old Ford Zodiac waited patiently for them outside the house. A glint of sun rippled along its radiator. It smiled. They got in. They set off for the funeral.

There was a ragged knot of black youths leaning against the walls of the old Moffat Street tram sheds. An old lady with a rusty pram and a half full bottle of cider squatted against the gates of the abandoned ropeworks of Flatman, Wrigley and Nutbrown.

And as they reached the ruined yards of the old locomotive works Uncle Mort commenced to tell Carter Brandon about Young Chocolate.

'He were a leading contender, were Young Chocolate,' he said.

'For what?' said Carter Brandon.

'The cruiserweight championship of the British Empire.'

'Oh.'

'I've seen all the greats, Carter. I've seen them all – Iron Hague, Jack Petersen, Tommy Farr, Len Harvey, Bruce Woodcock, Tami Mauriello, Nel Tarleton, Ernie Roderick, Gus Lesnevitch, Joe Baksi, Alf and Arthur Danahar, W. Barrington Dalby. But Young Chocolate had no peer amongst them. He were in a class apart.

'He were dynamite, Carter. He were right lissome. He were fast. He were powerful. His fists moved like greased lightning, like adders striking at a rabbit. He bobbed and he weaved. He were poetry in motion, were Young Chocolate.'

'Then why wasn't he cruiserweight champion of the British Empire?' said Carter Brandon.

'He didn't turn up for the fight,' said Uncle Mort.

'What?'

'The bugger were in the pub supping with me and me dad.'

'Why?'

'Oh, that's another story, is that,' said Uncle Mort.

They arrived at the church.

It was gaunt.

It stood in the centre of a rubble of terraced houses reduced to their smouldering foundations.

It was soot-stained and streaked.

A hearse stood outside. Three men in shabby black coats leaned against it smoking cigarettes from the backs of their hands.

'Turned up then, has he?' said Uncle Mort.

'Who?' said a man with flaky egg stains down the front of his shiny grey jacket.

'Young Chocolate, pillock,' said Uncle Mort.

'Oh aye?' said the man nipping out his cigarette between his thumb and forefinger and placing it behind his right ear. 'They're putting the finishing touches to him now.'

He nodded towards the church.

'Oh, it's nearly over, is it?' said Uncle Mort.

'I hope so,' said the man. 'I've a cage bird and poultry show to organise this afternoon.'

'Oh aye?' said Uncle Mort. 'And is there a class for Norwich canaries?'

'No,' said the man.

'Bloody typical of life these days,' said Uncle Mort.

There was a steady rumble of heavy lorries from the motorway viaduct which rainbowed the sky at the back of the church.

Two firemen in thigh-length boots prodded at a hydrant and a lazy-slippered woman sloppered by carrying a black dog under her arm.

Presently the three men adjusted the buttons of their coats, eased their crutches and trudged into the church.

'We'll not go in now,' said Uncle Mort. 'It's like the pictures, you see – it's daft to go in right at the end of the performance.'

The doors of the church opened and three bearers walked sombrely to the hearse carrying the coffin lop-sided on their shoulders. Resting on the lid was a small bouquet of pink roses arranged in the shape of a gum shield.

'By God, he's shrunk, has Young Chocolate,' said Uncle Mort. 'Look at the state of him. Look at the size of his coffin. It'd be just right for keeping cigars in.'

'Mm,' said Carter Brandon.

'He used to be a man mountain in the days of his prime, did Young Chocolate,' said Uncle Mort. 'He were as high as a trolley bus and he'd biceps like bags of cement. And look at his coffin now. It's as though they was burying a wizened wisdom tooth.'

A bent shuffle of mourners dribbled out of the church.

They watched with vague, watery eyes as the back of the hearse was slammed shut.

The man with the egg-stained jacket said:

'Right then, are we all set?'

'What for?' said one of the mourners.

'The burial, you daft bugger.'

The man consulted with his fellow mourners. Then he turned and said:

'We'll go to the pub first. We can always bury him later.'

And with that the limp gaggle of mourners shuffled off to the pub which faced the church belligerently on the opposite corner of the rubbled square.

'Selfish bloody sods,' said the chief bearer. 'I'll never get my prospectus out in time now.'

He joined his colleagues in the front seat of the hearse and they commenced to eat their sandwiches out of sliced loaf wrappings.

'What shall we do now?' said Carter Brandon.

'We'll join them for a pint,' said Uncle Mort. 'On occasions like this, Carter, you've got to swallow your principles and put on your religious hat.'

They went into the pub.

There was one sour bar.

There was a coke fire.

It was out.

'Two pints of malt beer,' said Uncle Mort to the landlord.

'Hold your horses, can't you?' said the landlord. 'I've got a rush on here and I've just had a stroke last Easter.'

'Hard luck,' said Uncle Mort. 'Do you do sandwiches?'

'No,' said the landlord. 'Not since the wife died. I wouldn't want to sully her memory.'

They took their pints of malt beer and sat by the silent coke fire.

They looked around.

The woman with the slippers and the black dog under her arm sat on an ill-tempered stool at the bar. A cockatiel with a bald, raw breast hunched itself into a corner of a cage next to the till.

And in the deepest depths of the room next to the back yard door sat the mourners.

They were silent. They were elderly. They were seven in number. They were male.

Bent backs. Bald heads. Clawed hands. Shrivelled top

coats. Thin shoes. Scrawny socks.

'By God, look at them, Carter,' said Uncle Mort. 'Giants.'

'What?' said Carter Brandon.

'The sporting heroes of my youth, every man jack of them,' said Uncle Mort. 'The true cocks of the North, Carter. The men who gave us hope and promise. The men who thrilled us and kept our pride alive in the dark days of our suppression and exploitation.'

'Oh aye?' said Carter Brandon, and he half hid a yawn in the gloom of his right armpit.

Uncle Mort pointed at an old man, who was raising his pint pot to his lips with two tightly clenched fists and spilling the liquid down the front of his sagging black trousers.

'Fighting Spofforth,' he said. 'The best welterweight the North ever produced. A killer, Carter. A wild pugilistic fury with dynamite in his hands.'

Fighting Spofforth abandoned the task of applying the glass of beer to his lips and concentrated instead on prodding his nostrils with a spent match from the ashtray.

Uncle Mort pointed to another mourner. He had a buckled, flimsy chest and a large, black, bakelite hearing aid.

'Ollie Woodhead,' he said. 'The Human Arrow. In his day the fastest sprinter in the North bar none. He'd have won the Powderhall Sprint dead cert, if he'd not been drunk on bad whisky.'

He picked out the other ancient drinkers in their turn.

'Guy Furnival, the dirtiest speedway rider who ever trailed his leg in the cinders at Odsal Stadium.

'Ernie Mumby and Victor Colclough, the finest breeders of whippets ever to don drinking boots this side of the Pennines.

'Nathan Wagstaff, warned off the Turf sine die for biting the bollocks of the winner of the Manchester November Handicap in '27.'

'He bit the jockey?' said Carter Brandon.

'No,' said Uncle Mort. 'The horse.'

He nodded at an old man, who was sniffing the cuff of his ginger Harris tweed jacket and scratching the wrinkled bone of his chin.

'Marcus Potts,' he said. 'The greatest of them all.'

'And what did he do?' said Carter Brandon.

'I don't know,' said Uncle Mort. 'They never told us.'

He sighed and fetched two more pints of malt beer from the bar.

'You know, Carter,' he said. 'It doesn't half touch me to the quick to see all these towering giants of our history turning out to do homage to Young Chocolate. I've never seen such a gathering from the Hall of Fame. I've never ever been so close to the heroes of my past.'

'Why don't you go and talk to them then?' said Carter Brandon.

'No, Carter, no,' said Uncle Mort. 'People like us don't talk to exalted creatures like them. We just sit in cold snug bars and pull them to pieces in private.'

Presently Fighting Spofforth fell asleep and began to dribble softly down his chin. Ollie Woodhead ordered himself a double whisky, and Marcus Potts took out his dentures and wiped them on the front of his maroon silk shirt.

'By God,' said Uncle Mort. 'It would warm the cockles of Young Chocolate's heart, if he could see all this lot.'

'Mm,' said Carter Brandon. 'Why did they call him Young Chocolate by the way?'

'Because he was as black as the ace of spades,' said Uncle Mort. 'He were the first nigger I ever set eyes on in the whole of my life.

'He came to live in digs next door to me mum and dad. Well, the landlady didn't look after him. She didn't feed him proper. She didn't give him his natural diet. So he used to come to us and me mother gave him special meals suited to his requirements.'

'What were they?' said Carter Brandon.

'Boiled bones and bananas,' said Uncle Mort.

'Mm.'

'You see, Carter, in them days we wasn't prejudiced against nig-nogs in the North,' said Uncle Mort. 'Well, there weren't enough of them about to make thoroughgoing bloody nuisances of themselves with their over long arms and their lazy arses and their fast bowling in public. Young Chocolate were just like one of us. Except for one thing.'

'What was that?' said Carter Brandon.

'He was a homo,' said Uncle Mort.

'What?'

At that moment the chief bearer opened the door of the bar and said at the top of his voice:

'Look. Do you lot want to bury this bugger or don't you? If I don't get this hearse back soon, I'll have to pay extra on the rental.'

The elderly mourners looked at each other. Nathan Wagstaff turned his head away and examined the small print on his bus pass. Guy Furnival took out a large bottle of white medicine from the inside pocket of his raincoat, sniffed it and put it back again. At length Marcus Potts spoke.

'Do you think you could manage without us?' he said. 'You see, there's still a good two hours of supping time left, isn't there?'

The chief bearer threw his head back, stamped his foot, flicked his shoulders and left the pub, slamming the door fiercely behind him.

'Come on, Carter,' said Uncle Mort. 'We can't let him go off to eternity without someone to see him on his way. He might not turn up on time.'

They hurried to the old Ford Zodiac and fell into line behind the hearse, which trailed a veil of sickly blue smoke.

The journey did not take long.

They came to a small cemetery on the side of a hill.

The vicar held a prayer book in one hand and a nasal inhaler in the other.

Uncle Mort threw a handful of coal black gritty soil on top of the coffin of Young Chocolate.

'Quite appropriate really,' he said.

The grave diggers appeared from the back of a tin shack and began to fill in the cowering hole. Their breath smelled of beer.

Uncle Mort and Carter Brandon sat on a headstone dedicated to the memory of Eliza Hardstaff and her cousin, Alderman Hardstaff, and lit up cigarettes.

'There's just one thing puzzling me,' said Carter Brandon.

'What's that?' said Uncle Mort.

'Why didn't Young Chocolate turn up for his championship fight?'

'Well, Young Chocolate had this crucial defect in his armament for a boxer,' said Uncle Mort.

'What was that?'

'He didn't like hurting people.'

'What?'

'He couldn't stand inflicting pain. And he hated the sight of blood.'

'Then why did he become a professional boxer?'

'Because they wouldn't give him a job on the trams owing to his colour.'

'I see,' said Carter Brandon. 'They thought he'd frighten the passengers, did they?'

'No,' said Uncle Mort. 'They didn't think he'd be able to work the points.'

The grave diggers finished filling the hole and returned to their tin shack. A factory siren hooted. A pigeon puffed out his breast and cooed and strutted in front of its mate.

Carter Brandon yawned.

'You still haven't told me about the fight,' he said. 'You've not told me why he was in the pub supping with you and your dad. You've not told me what happened to him after.'

Uncle Mort nodded.

'I know,' he said. 'It doesn't seem important now, does it?'

94

'No,' said Carter Brandon.

They eased themselves off the headstone and paused for a moment in front of the fresh grave.

'You've not told me why he was a homo neither,' said Carter Brandon.

'Shush, Carter, shush,' said Uncle Mort. 'Angels have ears, you know.'

They walked slowly to the cemetery gates. Just before they got into the car, Uncle Mort grasped hold of Carter Brandon's arm tightly and said:

'Don't ever say owt about Young Chocolate being a homo, will you, lad?'

'Why?' said Carter Brandon.

'Well, we're not supposed to have homos in the North of England,' said Uncle Mort. 'We leave that sort of thing to them buggers in the South.'

DARK, SATANIC WRITER

DO YOU KNOW the one place I detest more than anywhere else on the face of this earth, Carter?' said Uncle Mort.

'No,' said Carter Brandon. 'Where?'

'Liverpool,' said Uncle Mort. 'Where else?'

'Mm,' said Carter Brandon. 'If that's the case, shall we go there for the day?'

'Great idea, lad,' said Uncle Mort. 'They say purgatory can be quite interesting provided it's in small doses. It's rather like listening to Lulu on the wireless with her squeaky voice.'

'Mm,' said Carter Brandon.

Uncle Mort took three slices of black pudding from his breakfast plate, carefully wiped the grease off them on the edge of the tablecloth, wrapped them in his handkerchief and stuffed them up the sleeve of his jacket.

'You never know, Carter,' he said. 'They might come in

handy as iron rations, or something to put in the petrol tank if the car breaks down, the bastard.'

They put on their coats and stepped outside.

There was a gale blowing.

Uncle Mort had to cling on to his cap as he fought his way to the old blue and cream Ford Zodiac.

The pink blizzard of cherry blossom swirled about them as they pulled away from the kerb. A metal dustbin lid clattered crazily down the centre of the road in front of them and then bounded off down the hill in great hops and whoops. Rooks were flung in black tatters above their nests.

'Looks like there's a bit of a breeze getting up,' said Uncle Mort.

'Mm,' said Carter Brandon, fighting with the steering wheel as a gust of wind hurled itself at the flanks of the car from a gap in a newly-crumpled section of hoarding.

Uncle Mort chuckled.

'It'll be a bloody sight worse in Liverpool,' he said. 'It'll be really copping it there. Serve it right too.'

He chuckled again.

Carter Brandon shot him a swift, angry glance.

'So what have you got against Liverpool then?' he said.

'The people,' said Uncle Mort.

'What?'

'The people. I can't stand them,' said Uncle Mort. 'All that incessant talking. All that relentless cracking of funny jokes. All that unrelieved friendliness. All that smiling and laughing. It's an affront to the North, is that.'

'Pardon?'

'They give us all a bad name behaving like that,' said Uncle Mort.

'Why?'

'Because we don't behave in that manner in the proper North,' said Uncle Mort. 'We're indigenous as nature intended.'

'What the hell are you talking about?' said Carter Brandon, struggling with the wheel again as the gale clawed the roof of the car and tried to heave it towards the iron stanchions of the canal bridge.

'I'm talking about the racial impurity of the people of

Liverpool, Carter,' said Uncle Mort. 'That's why they're not true Northerners like us. They're half-castes – an unrelieved mixture of Micks, Taffies, Chinamen with cleavers and women who look like Cilla Black.'

'Bollocks,' said Carter Brandon.

'It's not, Carter. It's not,' said Uncle Mort. 'It's been the death of the reputation of the North of England, has Liverpool.'

'Why?'

'Because it's been too bloody successful by half,' said Uncle Mort, scowling and tugging at the peak of his cap. 'All them comedians making people laugh regardless. All them pop groups making people happy despite themselves. Them two football teams winning everything what's going. Liverpool and Everton! They make me sick. What have they got that Witton Albion and Stalybridge Celtic haven't got?'

'You what?' said Carter Brandon.

'You wouldn't know, Carter,' said Uncle Mort. 'They was long before your time, like rickets, misery and Congleton Town.'

Carter Brandon swerved to avoid a roof slate whipped across their prow by the wind. He looked through his driving mirror and saw it crash into the plate glass window of an Indian grocery stores.

'And that's another black mark against Liverpool – the Grand National,' said Uncle Mort. 'All them bloody horses jumping their guts out on telly just so Desmond Lynam's got an excuse to wear his funny sports jackets. Diabolical, Carter. He should be stopped by the RSPCA.'

'Mm,' said Carter Brandon.

'Then you've got the River Mersey. What's so special about that? Is it any wetter than the River Irwell? Is it any more glamorous than the Aire and Calder? Why has no one ever wrote a song entitled "Ferry Across The Yorkshire Ouse"?'

Carter Brandon shook his head and smiled to himself.

'It's a real mystery, isn't it?' he said.

'No, it's not,' said Uncle Mort. 'It's because them buggers from Liverpool are far too cocky, Carter. They just crave notoriety. Do you know, the workers closed down the docks deliberate just so they could attain the biggest unemployment figures in the North. Anything to get one over on the rest of us.

'Bollocks,' said Carter Brandon. 'I like Liverpool. It's a grand place and so are the people if you ignore their catarrh.'

Uncle Mort scowled.

'You're just prejudiced,' he said.

He fell silent for a while, and then he said, after pondering deeply:

'Do you like Nat Jackley and Betty Jumel, Carter?'

'Yes,' said Carter Brandon.

'You would,' said Uncle Mort. 'Anything to be awkward. You're that side out today.'

The gale grew stronger as they climbed out of the valley and headed westwards towards the high pass with its angry reservoirs and its cold-shouldered crags.

'I like this gale,' said Uncle Mort. 'With a bit of luck it might have knocked them bloody birds off the top of the Liver Building by now.'

'Shut up,' said Carter Brandon, and he applied the brakes as they approached a police road block.

The old Ford Zodiac stumbled to a stop with a sqeak and a judder.

'What's to do?' said Carter Brandon to the motor. cycle policeman as he wound down the window.

'Road's blocked up yonder,' said the constable. 'There's a tree blown down on top of a bus.'

'Is the conductor all right?' said Uncle Mort.

'What?' said the policeman. 'You what?'

'Come on,' said Carter Brandon to Uncle Mort. 'We'll take the other road through the dales and cross over the top by Buxton.'

He turned the car and headed southwards.

'These modern day bobbies – they never know nowt,' said Uncle Mort. 'And as for Buxton – that's a right closet of a place, too.'

Carter Brandon smiled to himself, leaned back in his seat, and the warm-hearted old car bowled happily down the soft dales road, singing to itself through the grill of its radiator.

The river alongside was swollen. Moorhens scuttered

white-rumped in its sodden water meadows. A heron stood motionless, peering at its toes.

Carter Brandon waited patiently and contentedly behind a line of Jersey cattle and saluted the herdsman as the felt-footed creatures broke into a trot and wheeled into the farmyard.

'Bloody cows,' said Uncle Mort. 'They should be shot.'

'Most of them are,' said Carter Brandon.

They came to a crossroads with a red VR post box set into a dry-stone wall and an iron bench overgrown with ivy.

Carter Brandon was just about to turn left on to the mud-spattered main road, when Uncle Mort said:

'Let's not go to Liverpool.'

'Why not?' said Carter Brandon.

'I've changed me mind – that's why God gave me one,' said Uncle Mort. 'Let's go there instead.'

He pointed to his right to a sign which said: 'To The Museum'.

'A museum!' said Carter Brandon. 'What do you want to go to a museum for?'

'I feel like a good kip,' said Uncle Mort.

'You what?'

'I feel like a good kip,' said Uncle Mort. 'Listen to me, Carter. These days there's only two places where a man can be assured of getting a good kip in peace and quiet with no disturbance – a museum or watching Preston North End play Darlington.'

Carter Brandon shrugged his shoulders.

'Please yourself,' he said. 'I'm not mithered either road what we do.'

He followed the signpost down a narrow country lane overhung with horse chestnuts and presently came to a cluster of low mill buildings with three high chimneys and a race rushing beneath a sombre and silent water-wheel.

There was a small gravelled yard enclosed by a low chain fence.

Parked on it, wheelless and asquat on wooden railway sleepers, was a steam lorry with the iron door of its open cab creaking back and forth in the gale.

There was a rusting threshing machine and a sagging

101

signal gantry.

A large sign above the arch of the main entrance proclaimed: 'The W. Tidy Museum of Living Northern Life'.

They got out of the car.

The wind snapped at their coat tails.

Uncle Mort climbed carefully over the low chain fence and patted the cab of the steam lorry affectionately.

'Noisy mucky things they was,' he said. 'I once saw one of them run over a policeman in Halifax.'

'Well, what else do you expect from Halifax?' said Carter Brandon.

He led Uncle Mort through the main entrance and into a large cobbled courtyard.

He looked around.

There was a straggle of unidentifiable and extremely large pieces of machinery. There was a single-decker Kingston-upon-Hull Corporation bus with no roof.

There was a selection of metal advertising signs nailed to the brick wall of a storage shed. 'Wills Superfine Shag', said one. 'Midnight Flake. 4d. per ounce. Perfection', said another.

Uncle Mort coughed in sympathy.

He walked slowly to a broken-backed motor cycle sidecar half-covered in tarpaulin. He was just about to sit in it, when a voice bellowed:

'Get your arse off that.'

They turned.

There was no one to be seen.

'Bugger off,' said the voice. 'Can't you see this place is closed, you bastards?'

'That must be the curator,' said Uncle Mort to Carter Brandon, and he took off his cap and bellowed at the top of his voice: 'Don't be a pillock. Open up. We want to use your bogs.'

There was silence for a moment.

Then a door opened at the farthest end of the courtyard and a small man burst out. He was bald and elderly. He had a limp and his face was scarlet with rage.

'Look, I'm warning you,' he said. 'If you don't vacate these premises immediately I'll ...'

He stopped dead in his tracks and shook his head with astonishment.

'Good God,' he said. 'It's you.'

Uncle Mort slapped his cap hard against his thigh.

'And it's you, too,' he said. 'Harry Hardcastle. What are you doing here?'

'I'm the caretaker,' said Harry Hardcastle. 'No one wanted to do it, so they forced it on me.'

'Well, you can't get better credentials for an important job than that, can you?' said Uncle Mort.

The two men stepped forward and shook hands warmly.

'By hell, Harry,' said Uncle Mort. 'It must be years and years since we last saw each other. I thought you'd copped your lot at the last big offensive. Was it the Somme or the Rotherham Old Comrades' Christmas Social?'

'Rotherham Old Comrades,' said Harry Hardcastle. 'I ate an infected trifle.'

'And did you get better?' said Uncle Mort.

'So they told me at the time,' said Harry Hardcastle.

Uncle Mort introduced his nephew to his old comrade, who smiled and said:

'Well then, what brings you here?'

'We've come for a kip,' said Uncle Mort.

'Well, that's all right then,' said Harry Hardcastle. 'I thought you'd come for some frivolous purpose.'

He led them across the courtyard and through the door he had burst out of so belligerently.

They stepped into a kitchen.

There were damp patches on the walls and strips of fly paper hanging from the gas mantles.

There was a brown stone sink, a single cold water tap and a warped, slimy wooden draining board.

There was a dresser, a meat safe, a large scrubbed kitchen table and two scuffed leather armchairs in front of a black-leaded range.

'This'll do champion, Harry,' said Uncle Mort. 'I'll have me kip here.'

'You can't,' said Harry Hardcastle.

'Why not?'

'This is one of the exhibits.'

'What?'

'This a full-scale genuine reproduction of a typical Northern working-class kitchen. We had it made special in fibreglass at Basingstoke.'

Uncle Mort looked at Carter Brandon despairingly.

The old brass-bound postman's clock struck eleven.

'Do you want showing round now you're here?' said Harry Hardcastle.

'Oh yes please,' said Carter Brandon.

Uncle Mort scowled.

'You would,' he said. 'I told you you was that side out this morning.'

But the scowl left his face instantly when his old friend showed them into the next room.

There was a bar counter with two pump handles, proud and erect.

The floor was covered in springy sawdust. Cast iron spittoons stood on either side of a brass-fendered fire. There was a long narrow table with benches on either side.

'Marvellous, Harry. Just what the doctor ordered,' said Uncle Mort. 'We'll have two pints of your best beer and you can take for a small whisky for yourself.'

Harry Hardcastle shook his head and yawned sheepishly.

'Don't tell me,' said Uncle Mort. 'It's another of your bloody exhibits, is it?'

'No,' said Harry Hardcastle. 'But it's strictly temperance. We're only allowed to serve dandelion and burdock and sticks of liquorice root.'

Uncle Mort clicked his tongue.

'Come on, Carter,' he said. 'Let's see if we can find the funeral parlour. They usually let you sleep undisturbed there.'

They stepped out of the bar and walked down a long gloomy corridor lined by glass-topped cabinets.

Carter Brandon glanced casually into them. In one there was a collection of vintage back collar studs. In another was a selection of stirrup pump adaptors. And in another was a display of early Northern stapling machines.

'Very redolent, Carter,' said Uncle Mort.

'Smashing,' said Carter Brandon, lingering in front of a

cabinet containing a comprehensive collection of parrots' toenails from the South Yorkshire coalfield.

'Come on, lad,' said Harry Hardcastle. 'There's much more better to be seen than that lot.'

He led them into an airy hall with large glass fan-lights, and there in the centre of the floor was an exhibit which made their eyes water with ecstasy and their hearts throb with excitement – a quarter scale model of the cricket pavilion at Bramall Lane.

'By God, Harry, that's a sight for sore eyes,' said Uncle Mort. 'The memories it brings back. Miller and Lindwall in full flood. Hutton stroking the ball majestically through the covers. Freddie Trueman knocking the stuffing out of them bastards from Lancashire. Aye, many's the good kip I've had in there.'

'Well, you can't have one now,' said Harry Hardcastle. 'You're not to the correct scale.'

They looked inside the windows of the pavilion.

It was perfect to the minutest detail. Everything was precisely to scale – the pork pies in the members' dining room, the groundsman's bicycle pump next to the indoor space invader machines, the working model of Brian Close using the visitors' urinals.

'Smashing,' said Carter Brandon. 'Bloody smashing.'

They passed through the Gallery of Northern Culture with its displays of used pumice stones, indelible pencils, tins of foot powder, stuffed Bedlington terriers, artificial limbs, North Western Road Car bus tickets and original snapshots of Albert Modley.

'I preferred Stainless Stephen,' said Uncle Mort.

They passed through the waxworks and Uncle Mort examined each character studiously and fastidiously.

At length he looked up with a puzzled expression and said:

'But all these models are of the same bloke, Harry.'

'That's right,' said Harry Hardcastle. 'They was cleaning out the BBC cellars at Leeds and they give us these figures of Don Mosey as a job lot.'

'Oh, Don Mosey, eh?' said Uncle Mort. 'I could have sworn it were Judith Chalmers.'

They moved on into the full-scale reconstruction of a

Workington public bathhouse.

The steam hissed and writhed. The carbolic scoured the roots of their nostrils. The heat throbbed at their temples and made their vests itch.

'Now this really is in full working order,' said Harry Hardcastle. 'You can have a bath, if you like.'

'No, ta, Harry,' said Uncle Mort. 'I always make a point of never taking my underpants off in a museum.'

It was then that a great grin came to Harry Hardcastle's face.

'Now this is our pride and joy,' he said, and he ushered them into a sound-proof room lit by soft red lights and furnished with canvas camp beds.

'Lie down,' said Harry Hardcastle.

Uncle Mort and Carter Brandon looked at each other suspiciously, but stretched themselves out side by side on adjoining camp beds.

'Right then, Harry, what happens now?' said Uncle Mort. 'Do you press a button and turn us into the Vernon Sisters?'

'Not quite,' said Harry Hardcastle. 'I press a button and bring instant delight to your olfactory senses.'

'You what?' said Uncle Mort.

'This is The Smell Gallery,' said Harry Hardcastle. 'In here by scientific process invented by real scientists we recreate the authentic smells of the North. Now shut up and get your conks working.'

He opened a black panel next to the door and pressed a red button.

There was a soft whirr and a purr.

And then Uncle Mort sniffed and wrinkled his nostrils. He twitched them rapidly. He breathed in deeply. A look of sublime delight came to his face.

'Bloody hell, Harry,' he said. 'I've not smelled that pong for donkey's years.'

'Wonderful, isn't it?' said Harry Hardcastle.

'It's perfection,' said Uncle Mort. 'Straight from the Garden of Eden, unsullied and pure – the unadulterated smell of tram drivers' gauntlets.'

Harry Hardcastle presented them with a further selection of smells and they lay back with their eyes closed and let their nostrils croon to the rich, redolent odours of dirty chip pans, wet spaniels, redundant gas works, tallyman's raincoats, overcooked pikelets and Wilfred Pickles.

Uncle Mort groaned with pleasure.

'Right champion, Harry,' he said. 'You haven't by any chance got the smell of stale mouse droppings, have you?'

'Why?' said Harry Hardcastle.

'Because it'll be just like my bedroom when I was a lad, and I'll be able to fall asleep knowing that all's well with the world.'

Harry Hardcastle nodded sympathetically.

'I've got something better than that,' he said. 'Come with me.'

He led them out of The Smell Gallery, up two flights of uncarpeted stairs, flung open a door, showed them into a small room and said:

'There. What do you think to that?'

Uncle Mort took off his cap and shook his head with wonderment.

'The ultimate, Harry,' he said. 'Now this is what I call the true heart of the North. Look at it – mucky, gungey, untidy, smelly and furnished in the most rampant bad taste known to man or beast. This, Harry, is easy the best exhibit in the whole of the museum.'

'This isn't an exhibit, you great pillock,' said Harry Hardcastle. 'This is my flat.'

Uncle Mort nodded slowly.

'My congratulations, Harry,' he said. 'I always said a good amateur can knock spots off the professionals.'

And with that he knocked a pile of decaying *Sporting Chronicles* from the tobacco-stained lumpy armchair, settled himself down, threw back his head and fell into instant, rumbling sleep.

Harry Hardcastle smiled and said:

'You're very welcome to stop here till he wakes up, lad. I'll have to leave you though. I've got some work to do dusting the poles on the collection of Mexborough trolley buses.'

'That's all right,' said Carter Brandon.

Harry Hardcastle rooted through a pile of old elastic knee

bandages and congealed string vests in the centre of the floor and from under it drew out a leather-bound book and said:

'You can read this to pass the time, if you like.'

'What is it?' said Carter Brandon.

'It's some diaries we've just acquired. They're going to be part of our literary section.'

'Oh, you've got a literary section, have you?' said Carter Brandon.

'Course we have, you great pillock,' said Harry Hardcastle. 'We've got some of the choicest literary gems in writing in the whole of the North of England here. We've the earliest known autobiography of Geoffrey Boycott – *and* we think he wrote it himself. We've a school report of Beryl Bainbridge's showing she came seventh in English literature and composition – pity she never improved, don't you think? And we've the first draft of *The Ragged Trousered Philanthropist* wrote by Roger Moffatt and Sheila Buxton.'

'Great,' said Carter Brandon.

'Right then,' said Harry Hardcastle. 'I'll leave you to it. Help yourself to a tin of sardines, if you can find the blow lamp.'

He left and Carter Brandon knocked a pile of defaced *Children's Newspapers* off the armchair and settled himself down to read the book.

It was entitled:

'*The Diaries of a Dark Satanic Writer* by Anon.'

They were written in green ballpoint and started thus:

'April 23rd, 1965.

'Another rejection slip. My 20th.

'What am I doing wrong? Why aren't I a famous Northern novelist like Stan Bairstowe? I've got an 'O' level in woodwork and everyone says I look the spitting image of Margaret Drabble.

'Maybe I should use double spacing on my typewriter.'

He read on:

'April 23rd, 1969.

'Another rejection slip. My 472nd.

'Maybe I should concentrate on being the second Philip Larkin.

'"They fuck you up, your mum and dad."

'But mine didn't. That's the trouble, perhaps. They gave me a very happy loving contented childhood – the bastards.'

He lit a cigarette and continued:

'April 23rd, 1974.

'Another rejection slip. My 473rd.

'I heard John Braine on "Any Questions" the other night. Maybe you've got to have a squeaky little voice to be a famous Northern writer.

'Will I ever get on "Desert Island Discs" and "Start The Week"?

'I spilled a bottle of Tizer all over my synopsis for a BBC radio short story last Thursday. I wonder if that ever happened to Margery Bilbow?'

Carter Brandon finished his cigarette. He looked in vain for an ashtray. He crushed the stub among all the other debris on the threadbare hearthrug.

He continued:

'April 23rd, 1975.

'Another rejection slip. My 908th.

'Granada finally wrote to say they didn't want my soap opera set in a pre-stressed concrete factory. I think they are right, because intrinsically and basically it has little human interest except for those "in the know".

'I think I'll send it to Yorkshire TV.'

Carter Brandon yawned.

But still he read on:

'April 23rd, 1980.

'Another rejection slip. A thousand up!

'How do you pronounce the Stoughton in Hodder and Stoughton? I'm sure it's things like that which make all the difference between failure and success in the literary world.

'Maybe I should enrol in the Brad Ashton Correspondence Course for Writers. I believe it did wonders for E. M. Forster.'

Carter Brandon skipped a few pages and came to the next extract:

'April 23rd, 1981.

'Another rejection slip. My 1,008th – I think.

'I think I am nearly there!

'A very nice lady from *The Dalesman* wrote to say that my

article showed "distinct promise".

'She said they hadn't got much scope for novellas about secret service agents having it off with women with big tits in Wakefield, but if I tried my hand at an article about early Yorkshire home loom weavers, she'd give it her "earnest consideration".

'Eureka!

'Great oaks from little acorns etc etc etc.'

The green ballpoint turned to red.

'April 23rd, 1984.

'Another rejection slip. My 2,458th.

'My green ballpoint pen has run out. I think it lasted very well considering.

'I still can't get the dialogue right for my piece on the loom weavers.

'If only I could win the Booker Prize, I'm sure it would give me some encouragement.

'I could have been Melvyn Bragg if only I'd got sinus trouble.

'I could have been Salman Rushdie if only I knew how to write English in a funny accent.

'I could have been Ted Whitehead if only they'd have invited me to be on "Kaleidoscope".

'I could have been any famous writer, if only I hadn't been me.'

Carter Brandon came to the last entry.

He began to read it, and he instantly sat up in his chair, tingling with excitement.

It went thus:

'April 23rd, 1986.

'Success at last. A letter of acceptance!!!

'Tomorrow I start work as an assistant on Dixon's home computer counter.'

Carter Brandon snapped shut the diaries.

Uncle Mort woke up.

'Shall we be off then, Carter?' he said.

'Hadn't we better say goodbye?' said Carter Brandon.

'No,' said Uncle Mort. 'I want to get back in time for the early news on the wireless.'

'Why?'

'To see if that bus conductor's all right. It's been worrying me all day.'

Carter Brandon smiled.

'I wonder if he looks like Margaret Drabble,' he said.

2084

I T WAS THE LAST DAY of Carter Brandon's week off work.

Softly during the night snow had fallen. It quilted the morning in silence.

There were no motor cars. Birds did not sing to the spring. There was no rustle of saplings.

'It's even shut up next door's parrot,' said Uncle Mort.

'Mm,' said Carter Brandon. 'I don't know why he keeps the bloody thing.'

'Simple,' said Uncle Mort. 'It's a good antidote to his wife.'

The city was caught in the snare of the snow.

It could not move.

Beyond its stealthy boundaries the high moorlands and the placid dales turned in on themselves and brooded.

And far beyond them, where the North Sea grumbled and heaved its shoulders at fulmar-stiff cliffs, fog-horns boomed and bitterns in their reed beds shivered.

'I don't think they'll get much cricket in today, do you, Carter?' said Uncle Mort.

'No,' said Carter Brandon.

'Nesh buggers. They don't know they're born these days, don't county cricketers,' said Uncle Mort. 'In the old days of the North people used to pay to watch them, so they had to turn out regardless of the weather. Nowadays you can't drag folk to the games, so they spend all their time skulking in the pavilion, smoking opium and giving each other home perms.'

'True,' said Carter Brandon. 'Very true.'

They were sitting in the back parlour, marooned from the outside world with its surgical shoe shops, purveyors of fine wines and spirits and stockists of surgical requisites.

The morning paper had not arrived. Neither had the post.

The batteries had run down on the wireless.

'I feel cut off without the wireless,' said Uncle Mort. 'I wonder if they've had another earthquake in Peru.'

'I don't know,' said Carter Brandon. 'It's always on the cards, isn't it?'

'Aye,' said Uncle Mort. 'I like a good natural disaster, me. It makes up for all the disappointment when Manchester United have lost.'

'Mm,' said Carter Brandon.

'And have you noticed, Carter, when you get the first reports on an earthquake, or a flood or a drought, they always underestimate the deaths. It's always five or seventeen that's snuffed it, and you know bloody well it's not true.

'You know next bulletin they'll say it's a hundred and then a thousand and then you say to yourself: "Come on, you buggers, you can reach the two thousand if you try. You can break all the records if you put your minds to it." Have you noticed that, Carter?'

'Yes,' said Carter Brandon.

'Good,' said Uncle Mort. 'I'm glad to see you're taking an active interest in current affairs.'

Carter Brandon stood up, went to the window and looked out.

The sly tracks of a cat sidled the snow on the lawn in the back garden. Icicles hung from the eaves of the shed. Frost crackled in the whiskers of the upturned yard brush.

'I wonder what it's like out in the front,' said Uncle Mort.

'Very much the same as the back I shouldn't wonder,' said Carter Brandon.

'Aye, there's no variety in life in these parts no more,' said Uncle Mort. 'Thank God.'

Carter Brandon hunched his shoulders and plunged his hands deep into his trousers pockets.

He felt a damp, congealed handkerchief, half a treacle toffee and a crumpled receipt from the beer off.

'Having a game of pocket billiards, are you?' said Uncle Mort.

'No,' said Carter Brandon, and he turned from the window and said: 'It's my last day of freedom. Do you fancy a trip out?'

'In this bloody weather? You must be joking,' said Uncle Mort. 'It's your classic stop indoors weather, is this. It's a day to stoke up the fire, raid the biscuit tin and annoy your mother. Only a raving idiot would think of setting foot over the front door step.'

'Mm,' said Carter Brandon. 'Course we could always go down to the pub.'

'Right,' said Uncle Mort, springing to his feet. 'Now you're talking sense, lad.'

They went into the hall. Winter had wormed its way back. The draughts from under the front parlour door snuffled cold-nosed at their shins. The mat at the front door had returned to stiff-bristled hibernation.

Carter Brandon rooted in the cupboard beneath the stairs and produced wellington boots, woollen mufflers and bottle green mittens.

They sat on the foot of the stairs side by side and put on their winter garments, grunting and grumbling.

'I bet Captain Scott and his mates were like this before they made the final dash to the South Pole,' said Carter Brandon.

'Aye,' said Uncle Mort. 'But his mission weren't half so fraught as trying to reach the pub like us.'

When they stepped out through the front door, the chill breath of the wind tweaked the linings of their lungs and ran icy fingernails up the snuffles of their nostrils.

They coughed.

'Do you like Manuel and his Music from the Mountains?' said Uncle Mort.

'No,' said Carter Brandon.

'Good,' said Uncle Mort. 'I can't stand them neither.'

The pavements scrunched beneath their feet. They slipped and slid. They slithered.

The sky was bruised purple, but a brief snout of sun peeked above a moustache of jet black cloud.

At length they came to the site of 'The Whippet', where popular mine host and ex Green Howard, Bert Coleridge, and his better half, Enid, had held court and hot pot suppers.

Now it was no longer.

It had been burned down owing to fire and replaced by a new building with green-tiled roof and pink breeze-block walls.

It had been renamed 'The Sweet Rose of Yorkshire'.

'"The Sweet Rose of Yorkshire"!' said Uncle Mort. 'It's a contradiction in terms, is that.'

'Very true,' said Carter Brandon.

They went inside.

It was empty save for an unlit space invader machine and a flat-chested barmaid drinking a mug of tea.

'Do you want serving?' said the barmaid.

'Well, that's the general idea, missus,' said Uncle Mort. 'We didn't come out for the good of our health.'

They ordered two pints of beer in straight glasses with whisky and ginger wine chasers and made their way to the corner where there once had been a shield for the Buffs and a signed photograph of Ronnie Hilton.

Now there was a reproduction poster for Hercules bicycles.

'How are the mighty fallen,' said Uncle Mort.

In a spotlit recess of the wall opposite them was an ornamental bamboo aviary. They stared in silence at a cobalt blue budgie for a while and then Uncle Mort said:

'I wish I could stand on one leg and scratch me arse with me nose like that.'

'I don't,' said Carter Brandon.

'Do you want serving?' said the barmaid

'No,' said Uncle Mort. 'On sober reflection neither do I.'

And then gradually the pub began to fill up.

The customers were young people in the main, for the older folk had long since passed on through apathy or death.

Their talk was animated. Their eyes sparkled. They even smiled.

Uncle Mort scowled.

'I was once a young person many many moons ago,' he said.

'Were you?' said Carter Brandon. 'And what happened to you?'

'I realised the folly of it all,' said Uncle Mort. 'I realised the essential fruitlessness of being young.'

'So what did you do?'

'I took up crown green bowls.'

Carter Brandon bought more beer and whisky and ginger wine. The barmaid smiled at him and said:

'You don't remember me, do you, Carter?'

'No,' said Carter Brandon, and he returned to the table with the drinks.

By now the voices of the young people had grown louder. Most of them were from the Polytechnic which had been established in the former premises of the Fire-damaged Carpet Warehouse.

A young man in khaki combat jacket and baggy trousers laughed out loud and said:

'No way, Sue. No way.'

'Right, Wayne. Right,' said his pink boiler-suited companion.

'You see,' said Uncle Mort. 'They don't even have proper names in the North these days.'

'Mm,' said Carter Brandon.

'In my day we had real Christian names,' said Uncle Mort. 'You was trapped with them from birth and they created your character until you was buried in your grave. Once born an Ernest, and you was doomed to be an Ernest forever. Christened Norman, and you was destined to be gormless and hang dog till the day you died. Christened Albert and that was you done for as a pompous old git with hair growing out of your nostrils and a tarnished fob chain rattling on

120

your beer gut.

'But look at the names they give them these days. How can you take them serious? Wayne, Darren, Kirk, Tracey, Michelle. How can you make anything of your life with a name like that? Would you vote in an election for a bloke called Darren? Would one of them chinless wonders from the Royal Family be allowed by his mum to marry a woman called Tracey? Princess Tracey and Princess Michelle! Can you imagine it, Carter? It'd make us a laughing stock at the World Cup Finals.'

'Mm,' said Carter Brandon.

Uncle Mort drew Carter Brandon closer to him and pointed with his thumb at the young people behind him.

'And they don't know how to sup proper neither,' he said. 'They're a bloody disgrace to the North, them buggers.'

'Why?' said Carter Brandon.

'Well, look what they're drinking. Lager and lime and halves of bitter shandy. And they only have one glass. They make it last all bloody session, too. In my day if you didn't sup a pint once every ten minutes the landlord threw you out and barred you from his pub for life.'

'Times change' said Carter Brandon.

'I know they do,' said Uncle Mort. 'And not for the better.'

There was a volley of laughter and one of the young girls threw her arms round her boyfriend's neck and kissed him on the cheek.

'Bloody kissing in a pub,' said Uncle Mort. 'No wonder the beer pumps look so droopy.'

Carter Brandon looked across at the table.

A girl with ash blonde hair, straight nose and large rimless spectacles smiled at him. He smiled back.

She was sitting slightly apart from her companions. She was rolling a cigarette from a battered tin. The tip of her pink tongue appeared between her lips as she concentrated on her task. She had green eyes flecked with grey. She caught Carter Brandon's stare. She smiled at him again. He turned his head away.

'Take that girl yonder rolling her own cigarette,' said Uncle Mort.

'What about her?' said Carter Brandon, coughing and

hunching his shoulders.

'Cocky little faggot,' said Uncle Mort. 'She looks so bloody superior. Well, by God, Carter, she's got a right shock in store for her, I can tell you.'

'What?' said Carter Brandon.

'Old age,' said Uncle Mort. 'Look at her with her fresh face and her clean hair and her straight nose. In my day she'd have been an old woman by now. She'd have had wrinkles, sagging tits and a gaggle of snotty-nosed kids hanging round her skirts.'

Carter Brandon looked at her again out of the corner of his eye.

She was leaning back in her chair, smoking the cigarette and smiling distantly at her friends. She had slim white hands with sparkling fingernails. Her jumper was loose, but he could see the swell of firm breasts.

'But she can't delay old age and sickness, Carter,' said Uncle Mort. 'There'll come a time when Sebastian Coe will need a bath chair to run a four-minute mile. The day will dawn when Anneka Rice will need a fork lift truck to get her into her helicopters. Look at Prince Charles and his brothers – they've got all them detectives and armed guards hanging round them, and even they can't stop them getting bald patches on the backs of their heads.'

He drank the remains of his pint fiercely and whispered confidentially into Carter Brandon's ear.

'I know it's a bit of a chore for you, Carter, but just take a look at that girl with the straight shonk,' he said. 'Just look and you'll see old age grinning and smirking at you just below her skin.'

Carter Brandon raised his pint pot to his lips and looked at the girl through the bottom of the glass.

As he stared he saw her change into an old lady.

She had ash blonde hair, green eyes flecked with grey and slim white hands with polished fingernails. The jumper was still loose and the swell of the breasts was still firm.

He snatched the glass from his lips and banged it hard on the table.

'You see, Carter. You see, lad,' said Uncle Mort with a broad smile. 'Ravaged, eh? All wrinkled and scrawny. That cocky look wiped off her face, eh? Just like the rest of us, lad – permanently out of breath, chronically short of money and decrepit in every bone and sinew.'

'Give over,' said Carter Brandon. 'Bloody give over, will you?'

He went to the bar.

The youth in front of him was ordering a half of cider and a packet of pork scratchings. He took out a purse and paid for it with a finicky combination of coppers and five p coins.

Carter Brandon asked for two pints of beer and two large whiskies.

'That's better,' said the flat-chested barmaid. 'That's what I call an order.'

Uncle Mort smiled at him, when he returned to the table.

'Not a bad outing this, eh?' he said. 'You can't whack a good grumble and gripe for reviving the spirits, can you?'

'Mm,' said Carter Brandon.

The blonde girl smiled at him again.

'I look around me,' said Uncle Mort. 'And I think to myself after all these years what are we doing here? What's the meaning of it all?'

'Life?' said Carter Brandon.

'No. This pub, pillock,' said Uncle Mort.

Carter Brandon grunted.

The girl was reading a book. Once more the tip of her tongue stuck out as she concentrated. She had long legs.

'I wonder what'll it be like a hundred or so years on from now,' said Uncle Mort. 'I wonder what them young buggers yonder will have made of it all.'

Carter Brandon shrugged his shoulders.

'I suppose it'll all be very different,' he said. 'We wouldn't know it. Everyone'll be run by computers. You'll have space ships to take you from Hunslet to Hoyland Common. You'll get an A level in advanced philosophy just so long as you've learned to wipe your arse proper and all the babies'll be born out of test tubes on the bacon counter at Tesco's.'

Uncle Mort chuckled.

'No, lad, no,' he said. 'It'll not be like that. I've got faith, you see.'

'Faith?' said Carter Brandon.

'Aye,' said Uncle Mort. 'Faith in the old and tried values of the North of England. We'll not give in to the digital alarm clock that easy, lad.'

The girl snapped shut her book, stood up, nodded to her fellow students and made for the door. As she passed by Carter Brandon, her sleeve caught his shoulder and he picked up the scent of fresh-washed hair and yielding limbs.

He smiled at her, but she did not see him.

Uncle Mort took a sip from his double whisky.

'Aye, Carter, the rest of England'll be like you describe it in 2084 or thereabouts, but not the North,' he said. 'We'll never give in. We'll revert to type. All those things we hold most dear will return and flourish and bloom.

'Come 2084 and there'll be trams on cobbled streets. There'll be gas lights and public bath houses. There'll be oyster bars on street corners and UCP restaurants where they sell tripe in batter and cow heel stew.

'You'll have Stainless Stephen on the music hall. All the footballers'll wear baggy trousers and have partings in the middle of their heads. We'll pay for our pints in half crowns and threepenny bits. There'll be steam locomotives on the railway and machines on the platforms where you can buy a penny bar of Nestle's chocolate.

'It'll be Paradise regained, Carter. No women in pubs. No talking at mealtimes. No kids riding their bicycles on the pavements. None of them shopping trolleys with spikes what stick in your ankles. None of them portable wirelesses with loud music. None of them West Indian fast bowlers knocking the living shits out of us at Old Trafford on a Thursday morning.

'The North will be alive and kicking, Carter, with rampant gloom and despondency and the ultimate accolade of all – cricket played once more at Bramall Lane.'

'Mm,' said Carter Brandon.

Unnoticed by them the young people had left the pub.

They were the only two customers left.

A zebra finch trumpeted in the indoor aviary.

They had one more round of drinks.

As they stood up to leave Carter Brandon noticed that the blonde girl with the blonde hair and the long legs had left her book on the chair.

He moved towards it.

Uncle Mort took hold of his arm and held him back.

'I shouldn't bother, lad,' he said. 'It'll only be fiction. That's all young women understand these days.'

The flat-chested barmaid followed them to the door.

She put her arm in front of Carter Brandon and said:

'Are you still married to Pat Partington?'

'Yes,' said Carter Brandon.

'Pity,' said the barmaid. 'I used to fancy you something rotten when we was younger than we are now.'

They stepped outside.

The snow had melted.

There was not a trace of it.

Water gurgled in the gutters and splattered from the roof-tops.

Forsythia winked yellow and bold in front gardens. Daffodils nodded contentedly and thrushes sang.

They walked slowly back home.

'I wonder what she'll give us for tea,' said Uncle Mort.

'Black puddings and kippers?' said Carter Brandon.

'We can but hope, Carter,' said Uncle Mort. 'Man cannot live by belly pork alone.'

They came to the front gate.

Carter Brandon paused, breathed in deeply and sighed.

'Well then,' he said. 'That's the end of our travels, eh?'

'That's right,' said Uncle Mort.

'Would you like to do it again?'

'Yes,' said Uncle Mort. 'Provided the North's still here next year.'

When they went into the back parlour, they switched on the television news.

There had been an earthquake in Peru.

Bestselling Humour

☐ Picking on Men Again	Judy Allen & Dyan Sheldon	£1.95
☐ Carrott Roots	Jasper Carrott	£3.50
☐ A Little Zit on the Side	Jasper Carrott	£1.75
☐ The Corporate Infighter's Handbook	William Davis	£2.50
☐ The Art of Coarse Drinking	Michael Green	£1.95
☐ Armchair Anarchist's Handbook	Mike Harding	£2.95
☐ You Can See the Angel's Bum, Miss Worswick!	Mike Harding	£1.95
☐ Sex Tips for Girls	Cynthia Heimel	£2.50
☐ Lower than Vermin	Kevin Killane	£4.95
☐ More Tales from the Mess	Miles Noonan	£1.95
☐ Limericks	Michael Palin	£1.50
☐ Bodge It Yourself: The Beginner's Guide to BIY	Jeff Slapdash	£2.95
☐ Dieter's Guide to Weight Loss During Sex	Richard Smith	£1.95
☐ Tales From a Long Room	Peter Tinniswood	£1.95

ARROW BOOKS, BOOKSERVICE BY POST, PO BOX 29, DOUGLAS, ISLE OF MAN, BRITISH ISLES

NAME ....

ADDRESS ....

....

....

Please enclose a cheque or postal order made out to Arrow Books Ltd. for the amount due and allow the following for postage and packing.

U.K. CUSTOMERS: Please allow 22p per book to a maximum of £3.00.

B.F.P.O. & EIRE: Please allow 22p per book to a maximum of £3.00.

OVERSEAS CUSTOMERS: Please allow 22p per book.

Whilst every effort is made to keep prices low it is sometimes necessary to increase cover prices at short notice. Arrow Books reserve the right to show new retail prices on covers which may differ from those previously advertised in the text or elsewhere.